EDUCA
THE CHILD AT HOME

PERSONAL TRAINING AND THE WORK HABIT

BY

ELLA FRANCES LYNCH

NEW WEST PRESS

her sentences aren't long! Helps to read aloud.

ISBN 978-1-64965-155-6

New West Press
Henderson, NV 89052
www.nwwst com

Ordering Information:
Special discounts are available on quantity purchases by corporations, associations, educators, and others. For details, contact the publisher at the listed address below.

U.S. trade bookstores and wholesalers: Please contact New West Press:

Tel: (480) 648-1061; or email: contact@nwwst.com

CONTENTS

PREFACE

By writing this book in plain English it is hoped to reach two results:

Firstly. To open the preserves of pedagogy and child-psychology to those who, though naturally most intensely interested in the subject, are deterred therefrom by the forbidding phraseology wherein it has hitherto been discussed and presented.

Secondly. To help mothers to resume and do their sacred duty by their children instead of shirking it and delegating it to the school. All that I have written is based upon actual practical experience and study.

Like the long search for the Promised Land is the search for an efficient school, while the great opportunity of home instruction and education is ignored. Where shall I find the best school for my children? Teach them yourself the things you know and can do.

The need of practical explanation of home teaching has been demonstrated to me by the numerous inquiries which have been due to some knowledge of my own school work and also to articles which I have written at the request of *The Ladies' Home Journal* and other periodicals. Every lecture or address that I have given has been followed by requests for explicit and detailed lessons and definite plans. In many of these communications from mothers who are now teaching their own children I read with pleasure words like these: "I knew, after reading your articles, that I could do it. It seems so easy." Again, came letters from teachers who felt that such plans could well be carried out with small groups of children, and thus were established the neighborhood schools herein described.

A word of appreciation is due to Dr. Calvin N. Kendall, Commissioner of Education for New Jersey, under whose jurisdiction was carried on the first public school of individual instruction, and also to the many teachers who have labored with me to bring this plan into the public schools.

This book is dedicated to my mother and father, from whom I learned whatever good things are set down here.

Ella Frances Lynch

I

PERSONALITY AND OFFICIALISM

THE child's education begins even before the moment of awakening consciousness, when "baby begins to take notice." From then on his learning should be progressing every waking moment.

The mother, therefore, must be recognized as his natural teacher during the early and impressionable years. When it comes to the more formal training the mother, unfortunately, loses confidence in her own ability and feels it necessary, at no matter what cost to her feelings, to surrender her child to substitutes who are supposed to be better prepared for the task. The official interference with the freedom and sanctity of family and home begins.

One purpose of this book is to encourage mothers to resume and do their sacred duty by their children by retaining direct control over the education of their little ones. What these mothers need to realize is that a child is most unfortunate if his mother is not a better teacher for him in his earlier years than he will ever meet in the classroom. With proper individual instruction, essential at this period of life, every normal child can accomplish in four hours of daily work for four years results which are not now attained in eight years and eight weary hours a day. Only under right conditions can this be done. The great truth, long forgotten, but reasserting itself again more and more, all adverse influences notwithstanding, is that the home and the home only is the fundamental basis for all true education. The mother's lap is a more suitable place for early teaching than the most magnificent and best-equipped kindergarten on earth. Her belief in the worth and possibilities of her own child qualifies her as the educator par excellence. It is her sacred duty before God and man to live up to it. The best-intentioned teacher in the world can never feel the personal interest in her pupils that a mother feels for her offspring. The most willing child can never have in his teacher the absolute unshakable trust he places in his mother. Every good teacher realizes this and understands that there is a limit beyond which she cannot go and should not dare to go to assist the child. The holy of holies, forbidden to the professional teacher, is the mother's, and blessed is the child who has received his primary and primal instruction from that fount. Intuition, unflagging interest, an incentive actuated by love, helpful sympathy—all these place the mother high above the professional educator.

Many a mother feels and realizes this. Distrust of her own scholarship and teaching-ability makes her hesitate to assume the task. She should thrust aside her fears. I have never known, in all my experience, a child taught at home to read, write, or compute who failed to hold his own in school. In rare instances only did the mothers who taught their children rank high in scholarship. Moreover, the little one was fortified with that deep-reaching religious and moral training which no school can impart, and his future was brightened and assisted thereby beyond compute.

What I conceive to be errors militating against the child as an individual, under the modern system of public-school education, I have described in the chapters that follow. Why I consider them errors I have pointed out with such clarity as I could command. In whatever criticisms I have indulged I have endeavored to refrain from any more severity than I believe necessary to accentuate the value of the individual method of reaching the inner sensibilities of the child. I might, perhaps, embrace in a paragraph the whole argument for the revision of the modern school methods of teaching: "If a school is going to amount to anything as a preparation for life, why not make it lifelike? A life-work cannot be reduced to a mathematical equation, nor are men outside of the school-room walls foolish enough to think that it can." Mere stuffing the mind with knowledge results in a lethargy, maybe in absolute stupor. To educate properly, to nourish the mind, we must apply the laws of biology. A defect in education means a defect in mental and physical life.

One requisite of education is proper mental environment. The child has large ideas. He must have room for them. Until the public-school system has undergone the reconstruction work now promised by our educators, and the spotlight has been turned from the workings of the system to the needs of the child, the parents must take a hand in the education of their children.

In outlining a plan of home instruction this book deals but sparingly with the theory of education, and contents itself with marshaling plain facts and essential principles. Some chapters strike a new note. The chapter on arithmetic alone would justify the publication of the book. A steady adherence to the principles therein presented insures the child's becoming an independent worker, and in many cases developing the power and the will to pursue alone the study of mathematics. In presenting the arithmetic lessons I have followed a straight and unquestionably practical plan that has been tried and successfully used by other teachers.

The chapter on poetry marks the difference between natural and artificial methods. It shows that poetry, as the language of childhood, should constitute the foundation of the work. This fact, though not questioned by thinking people, has, so far as I know, not been recognized by educators in its bearings on mind development. A proper application of this one truth is likely to mark the difference between real success and a feeble imitation. We know, of course, that the schools make use of verses and short poems, but they persistently neglect the fine, long, continuous compositions, the mastery of which develops in the child the power of sustained concentration.

A third chapter dwells upon the qualifications of the mother as a natural educator. Home training during the first ten years means so much that, personally, I have come to regard it as paramount in education. The school at its very best can only be an auxiliary. It is, after all, nothing but a wholly artificial institution which is an outgrowth of the parents' shirking of their highest duty to unload it upon paid substitutes. Let once the majority comprehend that it is only by training the child at home, with church and school as auxiliaries, that an efficient instruction can be imparted, and the pressure of united opinion will have its effect in breaking down the walls of adherence to the past. With their downfall will go the fallacy of believing that education can be imparted in bulk as a grocer dispenses sugar and flour, or that fixed rules and formulas are vital to success.

The first chapters outline briefly what are accepted as the most striking evils of the present system of public instruction, and add suggestions for reconstruction. The remaining chapters give simple plans for teaching the child either at home or in the small neighborhood schools for individual instruction, that are proving such a success in different parts of the United States.

Like the long search for the Promised Land is the search for an efficient school, while the great opportunity of home instruction and education is ignored. Where shall I find the best school for my children? Teach them yourself the things you know and can do.

Since I introduced and successfully used this method of teaching, I have had a vast number of requests for explicit instructions and definite methods from correspondents, parents, teachers, and from numerous readers of my articles in the *Ladies' Home Journal* on "Can I Educate My Child at Home?" In many of these communications from mothers I read with pleasure words like these: "I knew, after reading your articles, that I could do it. It seems so easy." Let me add, "You never know what you can do until you try."

"What connection has your plan with the *Montessori System*?" I have been asked by many other mothers. The work, as outlined in the following chapters, though not necessarily presupposing Montessori training, will be greatly facilitated and furthered thereby, especially if the child has had such careful and thoughtful training from babyhood as any good mother, with the help of such a book as the Montessori System, is qualified to give.

That the rigid rules of study in our present schools apply to the mentally alert in exactly the same way as they do to those slow of intellect and the dullard is a discovery not original with me. Many wise and good men among our educators have deplored the barrenness of results from our public-school system. What shall be the remedy? Until there shall occur a general rearrangement of the school curriculum, individual assertion of the teacher and individual development of the pupil are impossible.

The keynote of this entire book is work, the formation of habits of work. So train the little child that, were he thrown upon his own resources as early as ten, he would know how to work, would have the desire to learn, the ability to pursue, even without a teacher, the studies that appeal to him. Part of this equipment should be the practical home training that will enable him even at that age to earn his keep. It is not too much to say that the child of ten, who lacks the habit of work, has not been given the kind of start that will lead to real education.

II

OUR PUBLIC-SCHOOL SYSTEM ON TRIAL

ONCE upon a time there lived a king who was very fond of fine clothes. He spent most of the day with his Master of Robes, changing from one gorgeous costume to another. One day two rogues came to him who said: "O King, we can weave for you the richest and most beautiful cloth ever seen, in rare and wonderful colors; therefrom we shall make you a robe such as was never worn by any prince. Besides its beauty, this cloth will have the valuable property of being invisible to the ignorant and to those unworthy of their office. May it please your Majesty to give us plenty of gold and fine silks, and we shall set at once about our task."

Without the least delay the king engaged them for their work, intrusting them with generous sums of gold and quantities of costly silk. These the rogues kept for themselves, but pretended to weave on their looms an invisible fabric of invisible warp and woof. Day after day they wrought at the magical task, consulting with each other as to color and design, until a goodly portion seemed completed. When the king came to examine his robe in the weaving he could see nothing, although the rascals pointed out to him the beautiful hues and texture. "Can it be that I am not worthy of my high office?" he questioned, inwardly, but at once went into raptures over the priceless workmanship. Then he called in his chief officers of the court. They, too, were overcome by the wonders of the magic weave.

Now came the day when the work was completed, the dress itself fashioned by the two rogues, and the king dressed in it to march at the head of a royal procession to church. All his subjects had heard of the king's robe and its magic properties. Although they could discern nothing, each feared to speak his mind and so to prove himself unworthy or else basely ignorant.

So the king marched ahead in majesty, while two courtiers carried his invisible train, until the voice of a little child was heard saying, "Look at the king; he has nothing on!" And all at once the scales fell from the people's eyes. His poor, shivering Majesty was standing there disgraced, shivering in his nakedness, crestfallen and disconcerted.

So it is with our people and our public-school system. On the wane are the days when rabid rhetoric, fulsome flattery, pretentious peroration were lavished in lauding to the skies the magnificence of that great institution. The pendulum has now swung to the far point opposite, until it has become the fashion to go to extremes, to pitilessly impugn what was once the rousing topic of the campaign orator, from the President downward. To-day our schools and our teachers are blamed for all evils, from the decadence of English poetry to the bad manners of our children.

And behold, who are the foremost to publicly confess that they no longer see that chimerically beauteous fabric woven around our public-school system, and to demand with iconoclastic fanaticism its destruction and reconstruction?

The *parents*, who find their children lacking in obedience, in manners, in discipline, in becoming modesty, in self-restraint, in will-power.

The *minister* who find the growing generation absent from church and chapel; unruly and irreverent at Sunday-school—or, rather, at the Sunday-school picnics and entertainments—without faith in God and without a holy fear of Him.

The *teachers* who, as the pupils year after year are promoted to their grades, find them less and less prepared for the work rigidly mapped out by the system, less and less boyish and girlish, frivolous, flippant, full of self-assurance and self-conceit.

The *pedagogues* who used to preach enlargement and extension, and now in sackcloth and ashes sue for retrenchment and curtailment.

The *statesmen*, who fear that our public schools do not help to train our boys to conform to the desired type of desirable citizens and our girls for the duties of wifehood and motherhood, but rather supply material for the ranks of atheists and anarchists and grist for the divorce-mill.

The *business men*, who are sadly in want of competent clerks and willing workmen, and cannot find for these positions boys trained to do faithful and accurate work, to put forth their best efforts, to understand that hard and patient work must precede success, to admit that respect and obedience are due to their elders and superiors, and to realize that they must first be good learners before becoming earners.

The *physicians*, who ascribe the many cases of spinal curvature, defective eyesight, and such ailments to the slouching posture of the children in school bench and desk, and to unsanitary conditions in the schools.

Now what are, by almost general consent, the reasons given for these criticisms?

The schools are overcrowded. One teacher is given the impossible task of instructing from forty to eighty undisciplined children simultaneously, of keeping order among them, and of stimulating them to work by moral suasion. Moral suasion, indeed!

The course of study is overcrowded. An effort is made to teach the children twice as many things—not twice as much—as did the schools of fifty years ago, although statistics do not show appreciably increased brain power through ever so many generations.

The course of study is not planned with a view to the different stages of mental development. Subjects are taught that are absolutely alien to a child's mind and must imbue it with such rampant self-conceit that it imagines it could have created the world in a much more scientific and acceptable way than the Maker.

The time allotted to those subjects—time not only wasted but misapplied for directly harmful ends—leaves insufficient time for such essentials as work, making an honest effort, reading intelligently, writing legibly and correctly, and doing correctly and speedily the simplest problems in arithmetic. While visiting a fifth-grade class of foreign-born children not long ago, they were found occupied with a test in history. The disheartened teacher explained that the period was being wasted on this test, although the children had no conception of the subject itself, and they could not even read the book intelligently. She added: "If we were only permitted to spend this additional period daily on reading and English, the children could be taught something, but we have no time for practical things. They cannot yet write the simplest letter, although 'letter-writing' has been on their schedule since second grade."

The inelastic and uniform course is shallow, conglomerate, and incomplete, devised with the idea of meeting the needs of children from every sort of home, of every degree of intelligence, blessed or cursed with every kind of inheritance, of every nationality and color.

The practice of our schools is not adequate to the *sine qua nons* of our deepest thinkers on education. As Ruskin says: "Modern 'education,' for the most part, signifies giving people the faculty of thinking wrong on every conceivable subject of importance to them."

The work is planned for the average child, irrespective of the fact that a child is either one child or another child—that you cannot generalize with things that are different from one another.

The bright child is not getting a "square deal." He is marking time, waiting for the lame duck to catch up.

We are frequently classifying as stupid, "not up to grade," the pupils whose intelligence is above the requirements, and who therefore fail to fit into the prescribed groove.

The rigorous grading and the rigid curriculum of the elementary school lead step by step to the high school door, although less than ten per cent, of the pupils will receive what is called a high school education.

The period of dependency is unnecessarily and unprofitably prolonged, so that a young man enters a business or professional career considerably later than he would in Europe.

Money is wasted in supervision and in paying high salaries to principals whose time is chiefly employed in clerical work. In this way not only are time, money, and energy wasted, but this exasperating dependency upon the ideas, fads, or whims of the principal, the district superintendent, the special supervisors of writing, drawing, manual training, and physical culture, and their respective assistants, and forced to teach from the angle she deems most gratifying to each of these superiors, the poor teacher finds her self-confidence so weakened that instead of growing stronger with each year's experience in the classroom she is becoming a less efficient teacher, if a more obedient time-server and politician. Said one teacher not long ago in her class-room, to a visitor: "There will not be a single supervisor popping into my room today; I am going to shut the door and teach the children something" A primary teacher visiting an experimental school recently, expressed the wish that she might be allowed to try in her own grade the plan for teaching reading—the plan laid down in this book. "Would not the principal permit you to try such a plan?" she was asked. "Yes," she replied; "but if the results at the end of the month did not fully satisfy him he would mark me C on the report, and my salary would be lowered five dollars. I cannot afford to risk the experiment." The only hope of promotion and increased salary lies in absolute conformity to the system and in unswerving devotion to routine.

So much emphasis is placed upon tests and examinations that teachers and pupils lose sight of any purpose of instruction other than to attain the passing-mark.

Instruction is so methodized, so analyzed and synthesized, that the human relation is lost sight of.

In regard to many of these indictments, it may be conceded that they are due to inherent weaknesses of the flesh. Many of them, however, show more and more pronounced symptoms of malignant diseases with each succeeding year. Yet even this is neither proof nor indication that sound public instruction is to become a thing of the past.

Without any attempt at exhaustive analysis let us consider one by one some of the factors militating against our common schools yielding better results. Beginning with the district school employing but one teacher, we find the morbid ambition to imitate the curriculum of the carefully graded city school, much as if a family keeping one servant aspired to the pretentious standards of the household maintaining twenty helpers.

Why should the one-room school with ten to forty pupils in a farming community be ashamed to stand forth in its true and purposeful character, proud of a noble past, yet living in the present, instead of giving to itself village airs, wasting strength and substance to attain the questionable prerogative of being able to label each of its pupils as first grade, third grade, full grade, behind grade, or graduated? The grading system, introduced in big schools to make possible the handling of children in large herds, and for no other good purpose, becomes a fetish, and is beheld in the light of unreasoning devotion. Even in the little and remote country school-house, wherein the number of pupils is blessedly restricted, the teacher, the school-board, and the county superintendent dream of converting it into a "graded" school. Keeping in mind that the purpose of the school is to teach the young how to harmoniously fit themselves into their surroundings, and to enable its pupils to use whatever capabilities they possess in any and all opportunities that may arise, or in the face of difficulties that may crowd around them, may it not be contended that the ungraded country school, with from ten to twenty children, can well become the ideal school—that its possibilities for good are limited only by the measure of the earnest, practical idealism of the teacher, conjointly with the sturdy, self-reliant, self-believing cooperation of the parents? In such schools and communities as these were trained the men of distinctive character, the men who were types, the men to whom America owes her greatness. With the futile effort to imitate city standards, the virility of the country school has departed, nor will it return until the day, now approaching, when we return to the plan of substituting the good of the individual for the demands of the curriculum, and the pupils again become the center of gravity.

The plan of the country school of fifty years ago, with its faults and shortcomings, more nearly approached the plan of individual instruction than is permitted by our over-nice, crammed modern course of study. Healthy boys and girls were given tasks commensurate with their strength; a piece of work completed, the day was not rounded out with "busy work," but by mastering another page of the arithmetic. Promotions were not scheduled simply for year-ends, but came on whatever day the ambitious student proved himself ready to do the work of the next higher class. The spelling-book, dictionary, arithmetic, and a reader that was a reader were the most important books. Such tasks as the memorizing of masterly orations, Longfellow's "Evangeline," and similar compositions, laid the foundation for the life-work of many a noted orator, writer, or statesman. Seldom indeed was the intelligence of the child insulted by tasks beneath its strength. His arithmetic was mental, and dealt with everyday problems – given the dimensions of a bin, and ninety seconds for thought, the boy of thirteen would tell you how many bushels of oats were contained therein. If he was told that Deacon West's haymow measured 20 feet by 20 feet and was 12 feet high, something less than a minute brought forth the approximate number of tons, worked out by the "rule of thumb." Furthermore, a thoughtful inspection of the same haymow would enable these boys to estimate the number of tons, without having recourse to actual measurement. Today the practice of drilling in mental arithmetic has nearly died out in such communities – in all communities

– chiefly because the results are not readily measurable by grade examinations.

If the truth were told, it is probable that the majority of dwellers in rural territory are short-sighted enough to lament the lack of fancied educational advantages for their children, and deplore the want of resources prohibiting their removal to the proximity of a village or city school. Mere bulk stands to most of us for greatness. The machinery of the fine, large school, devised solely for administrative reasons, seems to promise a product superior to that produced by the best efforts of the relatively simple, unsupervised, unpretentious workings of the district school.

But perhaps nowhere in our school system, from district school to university, is there an institution so totally apart from its immediate practical surroundings, so lacking in preparation for complete living, so void of the life that trains mind and heart and muscle, as the school of the small town with its mongrel course of study. Child life in the small town might well combine many of the best features of the rural community with the less objectionable characteristics of urban surroundings. The school that seizes upon such opportunities contributes to the molding of desirable citizens. Instead, we find in nearly every case that the end and aim of the school is to rush its pupils through a number of subjects having little relation to present or future existence, to be enrolled among the graduates from the high school. What comes after that has had little serious consideration, as if that "coming after" were not the most important phase of living. A young man recently graduated from a university remarked: "I have just commenced to wonder what it is all about. From the time I was six until I was eighteen, I was made to work as hard as I could for just one purpose – to go to college; and then for seven years I worked as hard as I could to get out again."

From kindergarten to senior graduation the child passes through a world of contradictions and strange unrealities that may well be named topsy-turvy land. He is taught to skip, jump, and plan games by a teacher who cannot skip or jump as well as her pupils, by a teacher whose inventive genius for devising games and "make-believe" is sadly inferior to his own. Lessons in nature study are learned from a book and pictures, while the great outdoors is calling him to study at first hand. One or two nature lessons a week or a sweet little stereotyped talk of a morning on the subject, or a rushing through the assigned topics for the year in the space of a week or two, to meet the requirements – no connection here with life. Subjects taught at the wrong time – fed on definitions and mathematics during the most imaginative early years, then later on with poetry just when the reasoning powers manifest themselves and demand different food. Mathematics are taught as memory subjects, and literary masterpieces for analysis. So many different bits of work are attempted in a day that much of the time is spent in starting and stopping, the distance between stations being scarcely marked. The contour of Africa is taught better than that of the native county; the pupils trace the course of the Amazon, but scarcely know, beyond the dealer's cart, the source of the village milk-supply. They learn of the hardships and intrepidity of the early settlers, but lack the willingness to persevere in a hard or distasteful task until success comes. They write wordy graduation essays on our foreign policy, that must be carefully pruned of misspelled words, incomplete sentences, slang and verbiage, before they are in shape to be read before a breathlessly admiring audience.

The picture is under-drawn. I repeat, that the training afforded by the majority of village schools is so needlessly complex and remote from life as to be a poorer preparation for living than is the ungraded district school, or the great city system with its overwhelming disadvantages, the latter being only a very complex part of a great complexity.

Can we harshly denounce the city teacher for giving a lesson on the dandelion with only a picture of the flower and a printed description as help? Our first feeling, instead, is one of pity for the children encompassed by an environment inimical even to the hardy dandelion, except in a picture. And the second, very likely, is an impulse of admiration for the teacher who could bring any semblance of the reality of nature into prison-like surroundings.

But charitable reflections must not stay us from a critical survey of the accepted pattern of standardized instruction, and from an equitable judging of its effectiveness in contrast with its possibilities.

In the beginning of this chapter are enumerated the findings of the critics on the public-school system in general. These criticisms apply in nearly every case to the unwieldy city system, and in a lesser degree to the town and country school, whose servile imitation of city standards has brought them low.

In the early days of the public school, when between teacher and pupil there existed a human and individual relationship, when the rights of the parents were recognized in the scheme of education, the measurement of a school's efficiency lay in the ultimate gain to the children. That was the day of close relationships insured by a small cycle–the child, the teacher, and the home–the day of the relatively unimportant adjuncts of school-board and superintendent.

The present epoch, however, from backwoods to city, marks a complete revolution in educational affairs. The old cycle is broken. The school is no longer responsive to the home. The child, the parent, and the teacher are but the relatively unimportant adjuncts of the monster syndicate, embodying less bulky corporations of school-boards and school-men.

It is one thing to establish and promote an all-powerful school system and quite another thing to promote the highest welfare of the children. The only real good is the good that reaches the child. One of the vital differences between the old cycle and the new monopoly seems to be in the relation occupied by the teacher. Put the teacher in the position of knowing that the parents have neither voice nor authority. Is it absurd to say that she will be influenced adversely to the highest interests of the child? The teacher soon learns that her future depends, not upon the quality of her work, not upon pleasing the parents, but upon kowtowing to those in power.

III

HOW TO DO BETTER

Do the critics of the public-school system bear in mind that there is frequently an unyielding difference between what is desirable and what is attainable? Denunciation of existing conditions is useless unless a remedy can be proposed. Would anybody be so rash as to believe that a reconstruction of the public-school system could be effected with the certainty, the scientific exactness, of even such a marvelous undertaking as the digging of an interocean canal?

But if, after patient consideration of the multitudinous allegations made against the present wasteful and ineffective scheme, we arrive at plans for betterment that have the thoughtful sanction of schoolmen, shrewd men of business, and other thoughtful minds, we may venture to set before the public our opinions as a contribution to the discussion of a vexing problem.

The general criticisms enumerated in the foregoing chapter may be divided into two classes. The one comprising criticisms of such peculiar local or deep-rooted nature as to make any attempt at betterment appear futile; the other comprising such defects as admit remedial discussion and immediate redress. Our criticism should mainly and properly be directed against the cumbrous city system, and in a lesser degree against the smaller organizations of town and country schools which draw these criticisms to themselves by attempting conformity to an artificial standard instead of making a courageous stand against it. Thus, the outlook is more discouraging for the city schools than for the aping town and country schools.

Now the city may not improperly ask the faultfinders:

Tell us how we are to avoid herding the children by thousands in each building? How meet the individual needs when we must supervise and direct teachers by the hundreds and children by the thousands? How avoid shoving pupils ahead in regiments whether or not they are fit for promotion when we must make room for the new ones entering in the lower grades? How avoid artificiality in teaching when the children have never experienced the joy of pulling a blade of green grass? And if we are not to have women teachers for the boys in grammar and high school grades tell us where we can find men teachers thoroughly trained and qualified for the work, who enter the teaching profession without the mental reservation to get out of it as soon as an extra one hundred dollars a year looms in sight?

Let us pass over these pertinent rejoinders, since the hope of betterment within a measurable time must be almost abandoned, and consider some of the other points, surely of no less import, that demand and admit mending, which, if accomplished, would tend to make easier the gradual solution of some of the distressing problems previously touched upon. Let us take up one by one some of those criticisms in the previous chapter, which can and may effect a speedy betterment.

"The course of study is overcrowded." If so many different subjects are undertaken that the direct result of school-training is lack of thoroughness, confusion of mind, and want of ability to discriminate between essentials and non-essentials, why not simply abolish the most objectionable? Is it unreasonable to propose elimination? When we consider the possibilities of improvement attendant upon such elimination the prospect brightens. Let us, for instance, take the case of the eleven-year-old children, contending with an assignment of eight lessons, in a school day divided into as many recitation periods, with perhaps an extra period each for singing, manual training or domestic art, and physical culture. Certain of these subjects are incontestably essential for children of eleven to study. Therefore, instead of juggling with each of them in its brief period let us choose the few of whose value there can be no dispute, and arrange the schedule so that long periods are given to those few. Undoubtedly, by teaching four instead of eight subjects a day, we obtain such desirable results as: thoroughness, continuous thinking, and a knowledge of what is really essential. Beyond question it is more profitable for a child to study one subject continuously for a whole hour than to be burdened with two subjects one half-hour each. Instead of short separate periods for reading and English these may well be taken as one subject. Naturally, we would expect that the piece of literature chosen as the basis of such a lesson be worth that much time and study. Such suitable masterpieces are still extant, the flood of grade readers notwithstanding.

Is any school system so massive, so complex, that the simplicity of this suggestion need appal its makers and guardians? Or is it only the ease with which it may be carried out that excites their suspicion? The suggested plan is for general application only. Details and methods must differ with the locality. Is the entire system disrupted if the principal grants permission to the fifth-grade teachers to throw aside the frills and see how much improvement they can secure in confining themselves to the teaching of spelling, reading, mental arithmetic, writing, and the ability to work independently? Let us not forget that for many children the fifth grade is the last year of schooling.

"The course is inelastic." The subjects, division of time, and text-books are practically uniform, not only in the different sections of the same city, with their heterogeneous population and needs, but, worse still, in all cities—North, South, East, and West. Where a school population is foreign-born the curriculum can well be adjusted to fit the case. Reading, spelling, and English should be taught the greater portion of the day. Arithmetic, which is acquired with so comparatively little effort by the young of many nationalities, may hold a subordinate place for a time. But the budding citizens cannot be given too much suitable English work, much of which may well be simply copying the reading-lessons. The principal of each individual school should have authority to adjust the course of study so as to meet the needs of his particular school.

"The period of dependency is unprofitably prolonged." By abolishing the grammar-school course and establishing a thorough, complete, and self-contained elementary course of from eight to nine years, each year's work being strictly consecutive and developing gradually and steadily the previous year's work, we should keep in view and attain the true purpose of common-school instruction, so to train our children that they will be fitted to take, in accordance with individual circumstances, their proper places in this working world, and, what is of still greater importance, so that if they have a desire to continue their literary education later on they will be fully equipped to do so.

Having thus provided for the many children who must and should go out into the world to work at fourteen or fifteen, we will consider the case of those few whom circumstances permit and whom ability entitles to prepare for university, college, the higher public offices, the management of large commercial, industrial, or agricultural business, etc. The secondary course should begin at the age of ten to permit of sound preparation for the university. That Latin and other foreign languages can be thoroughly taught in four short years of high school, not to mention the mathematics demanded by the college entrance examinations, will no longer be maintained by experienced teachers of these subjects, nor that they can be taught by those pernicious, quantitative, and impressionist methods that infest our modern teaching.

The secondary school should offer two courses – classical, for those who will go to the university to fit themselves for a learned profession; technical, laying more stress on modern languages and sciences, for those intended for other callings demanding a more advanced and extensive schooling, than that given by the elementary school. By such an arrangement, or by a similar and better one, a year or more would be saved in the preparation for the university, and the university authorities would no longer have to deplore the poor caliber of their students.

In his book *Standards of Education*, based upon the recent investigation of the elementary schools of Greater New York, Dr. McMurry recommends that such duties as are purely clerical and require no special ability should be performed by a clerk, whose salary would be one-half or one-third that of the principal. The principal should be a cultured teacher and pedagogue, not only a business manager and telephone attendant, and should actively discharge the duties of teacher in the highest classes in one of the most difficult subjects.

When a teacher has had reasonable experience in the class-room, and has displayed that enthusiastic zeal, tact, and intelligence without which her incumbency under any conditions becomes a most objectionable sinecure, withdraw the supervision and make her feel that she alone is responsible in that room for results. Confine the insistence upon close observance of method and system to the teachers standing in need of guidance, whose number, after the proposed change has been made, will become smaller and smaller. Put the teacher in a position of trust and responsibility, and she will rise to the dignity of her work and follow with reverence her high calling. Reduce the number of subjects to the indispensably necessary, and the teacher will see ahead a positive goal, knowing that she will be judged according to the gain the pupils have made in the power to do, in the mastery of fundamental lessons, rather than by the number she promotes to the next grade. As an incentive to eager, purposeful work the prospect of an increase in salary cannot rival the promise of an opportunity to project herself in an individual way in the life of her pupils, to be somebody, when she has proven her capability and worth.

"The course of study is not planned with a view to the different stages of mental development." In the effort to teach young children what ought to be reserved for an older age, subjects that call for reasoning-power and judgment, and therefore belong to the high school or a later period, have worked their way downward, step by step, until they permeate even the primary grades, often occasioning harmful incongruities between the matter itself and the language chosen to convey it.

On the other hand, the teaching of memory subjects, such as the languages, is long deferred, even to high-school years. Here again the remedy may be had for the choosing. Up to the age of ten the child is concerned chiefly with recording impressions, observing, forming habits, getting himself adjusted to a world quite new to him, storing up information that in later years will be reviewed in the light of reason. It is the seed-time, not the time of fruit-bearing. To determine what branches of knowledge and instruction are of least worth before the age of ten is a simple matter, and might almost be left to the children. It would result in the elimination of many subjects now occupying a place in the schedule to the children's detriment.

Nor should it be difficult to determine what subjects at this age are of real worth. Yet we are again confronted by what seems almost unattainable. Foreign languages, if studied at all, should be begun before the age of ten, when the memory is most active, the auditory and vocal organs most responsive to the formation and acquisition of new sounds. Although instruction in foreign languages has not thus far been considered a possibility in the primary public school, yet the way for such instruction may also in our country be opened in a time not remote. In other countries such instruction has been given for some time. The idea is suggestive of the group of studies fitting the period when the mind of the child is soft wax to receive an impression. This brings us to the presentation of a plan for the reconstruction of the primary school. Perfection is not claimed for it, nor completeness attempted. Its chief merit is simplicity and the certainty that experimenting along these suggested lines carries no harm to the little child.

In many localities the plan may be worked out in its highest form without additional cost. In others the additional cost will perhaps be one-fourth of the present cost.

Since the parents have permitted the primary school to arrogate to itself the special functions of the day nursery, the curriculum has of necessity adjusted itself to that purpose. Forty children are assigned to a teacher whose chief duty is to fill in the prescribed hours according to a fixed schedule. Children are in the classroom all day, not because they stand in need of all-day instruction, but partly because a teacher is supposed to spend so many hours in order to earn her salary, and partly because five or six hours is the usual length of a school-day.

The first year is the most important of the child's school life, one important task being the setting of right habits, and another the prevention of the forming of wrong ones. He must not form habits now that need to be broken later on. He must neither become an idler nor a dawdler, taking all day for the work he should perform in half an hour.

The first step toward reconstruction is to divide the first grade into four groups, so that a teacher will have not more than ten children in the classroom at one time. In the hour or two of instruction given to each group, far more of sound worth will be accomplished than with the entire grade all day together in a room.

The advantages of a small group for a short period daily, in conjunction with the liberty of action just urged for the teacher, are so evident as scarcely to require enumeration. It amounts to doing away with nearly all the difficulties in the way of successful primary teaching. Given a large room with not more than ten children:

There is little occasion for disorder.
The ventilation is easily regulated.
Individual instruction is permitted.
There is little difficulty in the way of good discipline.
The child comes to school eager for work, since he is not confined all day on a hard bench.

He looks forward to the coming of a new school-day, going home with reluctance.

He does not feel the friction of numbers peculiarly irritating to a young child.

Each day he can be made to work to the limit of his present capacity.

Progress can be marked by the teacher, not in the number of pages covered, but in the children's increasing power to work.

Every minute of the day brings happiness to teacher and pupil in the pure joy of the conscious doing of a good piece of work.

This fundamental suggestion of having ten pupils at a time for one and one-half hours each, beginning perhaps at eight-thirty and having but one section in the afternoon, offers this great advantage as well – that the class, divided at first according to measurable advancement or previous teaching of the children, as those who:

Have had no teaching.
Know the alphabet.
Can spell a few words.
Have memorized some poetry.

makes it possible to give teaching adapted to the needs of the entire group. This initial division, however, does not mean a permanent classification, as there is a more striking difference among children at this period in regard to their ability to learn than at a later time. This arrangement permits the exceptionally quick child to pass from one division to another, perhaps through the four steps in a single year, without the necessity of changing teachers. The child of seven who has had no home instruction and is placed in the eight-thirty division until the alphabet is mastered will do this quickly and move ahead through the classes to the afternoon division, which we will consider the most advanced, while some of the afternoon members have earned promotion to a division of the second grade.

Now, were it not for the fact that the school is regarded as a good place to send small children when their parents would get them out of the way, little more would have to be said of this general plan than that the children should go home when the short session is ended. This can be done in cases where parents are willing to care for their children the rest of the day. This part of the solution is not only a local but an individual problem. It must be dealt with by each community according to prevailing local circumstances. If the parents will not or cannot take care of the children after the period of instruction they must be kept in charge by the school, but not shut up in a close room, crowded into unnatural positions in benches, kept inactive for long hours. There must be playground and playrooms in charge of a sensible, matronly caretaker to see that the children do not get hurt. If large numbers are to be together there must be experienced supervision, but this does not necessarily call for the high-priced expert. The main point is that instead of pupils and teachers exhausting each other in the long hours under wrong conditions in the classroom, the little ones should be safely looked after outdoors or amid proper surroundings.

The National Playground Association could do no better work than in planning with various school systems this application of the children's time.

No hard and fast rules regarding exceptions or modifications of this plan are desirable beyond the insistence that the school must adjust itself to the community and individual needs – that the stimulus to change and betterment come from a knowledge of what is good for the children in that identical school and locality rather than from what may have been said to be the latest and most approved plan of the system.

First-grade children in the short session just advocated should make unmistakable progress during the year. In what this should consist will be pointed out in other chapters, but our present concern is to devise ways of making possible the individual teaching advocated in this book. Children taught for a year in groups of ten may, if necessary, be in groups of fifteen during the second and third years, spending two hours at hard work in the schoolroom. For the well-trained children between nine and ten, three-hour sessions, twenty in a group, will enable a teacher to do good work, and to give them all the instruction from books profitable to them at this age.

This plan has been carried out in both public and private schools with entire success. A county superintendent, in addressing the patrons of such a school in northern New Jersey, said: "Yes, your school does cost you more money than the ordinary school, but more is done for the children, and anything that represents a gain to the immortal soul cannot be measured in dollars and cents." This school did cost more money for the year 1912-13; but there were no repeaters, no neglected fringe to the class, no sick or nervous or discouraged children, but children none of whom disliked school, no cases of avoidable absence, no truancy. The work was accomplished each day in a reasonable length of time, while advancement was far more rapid than under ordinary conditions.

In the public schools of Mt. Lebanon, Penn., the first and second grades have been dismissed the last two years at noon, and their teachers are required to help in the teaching of higher grades during the afternoon, so as to provide a certain amount of individual instruction. The slogan of our schoolmen in discussing the reorganization of the schools is, "Elimination of non-essentials and greater flexibility in the conduct of the schools" They seem to think that they have done their part by talking, and except in rare and isolated cases nothing is done. Now does it not become the duty of mothers, until such time as the schools provide a rational scheme of instruction, to give their little children such teaching at home as by general consent should be given, until the schools follow this example and mend their ways? Mothers can do it better than the best teachers.

IV

HOME TEACHING, OR THE NEIGHBORING SCHOOL

GREAT pedagogues like Comenius, Spencer, and Froebel, great writers on education like Jean Jacques Rousseau and Jean Paul Richter, looked on pedagogy as an art. Their ambitious followers of this generation have tried to turn it into an exact science, with ever so many straggling offshoots like child-psychology, etc. As if a child's mind and soul could be vivisected like a poor dumb guinea-pig. The simplest difficulties in a child's education have been puffed up into so-called tremendous problems, so that the poor mothers, whose instinct and intuition alone can overcome these difficulties, have abandoned their offspring to the experiments of the professional pedagogue. Let the mothers take heart and reclaim their sacred privilege and duty to be the first and most potent factor in their children's education.

The pressing need for the reconstruction of the public-school system is intensified in the case of the primary grades. It is here that we earnestly plead for the mother's active help. All true reforms have begun at the bottom, not the top. The primary school is not only the logical place, but also the most convenient, for such a beginning. Moreover, it is the school through which the one hundred per cent, must go, the poor stragglers dropping out in ever-increasing numbers with each higher grade. But there are still weightier reasons which should compel us to immediate action. In the sensitive early years of childhood the complexity, the overcrowding, the deadening uniformity of a standardized system overwhelm and oppress. The Creator gave us our individuality for a purpose. To force all into the same mold is to thwart His purpose and to lessen the efficiency of our work in the world. In preferring our plea for the reconstruction of the entire system emphasis has been placed upon the needs of the lower grades, and a provisional plan, based upon the utmost simplicity of procedure, has been outlined. The conscientious mother of young children is confronted with these alternatives: either to proceed at once to reform the elementary school or else to teach her children at home until such a time as they will be mentally and morally strengthened to resist the evil effects of herding, of mass teaching, and of a complex plan of instruction.

While difficult to solve the problem of the multitude, the mother can, if she will, solve the problem of her own child. Quite different, indeed, is her problem from the teacher's. The latter, entering the class-room, says to herself: "What are my orders? How have I to deal with this grade? What does the principal want me to do? Does the superintendent approve of my methods? Have the children mastered last year's work? Shall I be able to get them promoted into the next grade?"

This leads us to ask: Why do people send little children to school? Why need there be such a thing as a rigidly prescribed course for children from five to eight or ten years old, any more than for children two years old? The chief reasons given by parents for sending young children to school are: first, sad to say, to get them out of the way; second, to give them an education.

"To get the children out of the way" is beyond question a legitimate excuse for the mother who must toil in order to feed and clothe her children; but the mother who looks upon the school and the kindergarten as an avenue to six hours' daily freedom from responsibility would do well to consider the warning: "Take heed that ye despise not one of these little ones."

When Froebel founded his first kindergarten he knew very well that the foundation of the highest type of education can best be given by the mother at home. But, feeling in his big heart a deep sympathy for the children whose mothers were incapable and whose homes were unsuitable to give that education, he founded his kindergarten as a substitute; which fact he himself emphasizes when he says: "Kindergartens are the most beautiful substitute for genuine family life." Thus it is manifest that his kindergarten was intended for poor children to whom are denied genuine family life, genuine mother's love, the genuine, strong, and safe corrective of a conscientious father's hand and mind. Is there, then, in our country no such genuine family life that we must turn, instead, to a substituted and misapplied kindergarten system? Is it not to be deplored that American mothers clamor for public kindergartens to relieve them of their responsibilities, and to so unload upon the state as a worrying burden what ought to be a sacred trust? In no other country are there relatively and absolutely so many kindergartens as in the United States.

"To give him an education." To do so is the bounden duty of all good parents. And it is the state's bounden duty to help. But give him that kind of educatión for which he is fit and which fits him for his walk in life. Yes, you want your small child to master the essentials of knowledge-getting. Very well; what do you do to accomplish this laudable object? You resort to the exceedingly wise and practical plan of surrendering him to the school, to be placed in charge of an overworked, underpaid woman with forty children in her care, to learn in five or six hours each day the reading, spelling, writing, and arithmetic which his mother could better teach him at home in a small fraction of that time ! Is this a promising beginning of an education? And when the experiment fails are you justified in placing the blame upon the school?

Why thrust the sensitive little child into the complexities of a modern school? Why make him conform to the artificial life and environment which is inseparable from the systematic manipulation of forty individuals receiving simultaneous instruction according to a predetermined and inflexible schedule? The power of logical thinking and the habit of careful work could no more be cultivated under such conditions than by the punctual daily attendance at a three-ring circus. The safe and fitting place for a little child is at home under the guidance and with the teaching of father and mother. Until the age of ten or thereabouts every child having a good home should remain in that home. It is the best place for teaching a child during the first ten years of his life. The training he receives from God-fearing parents will do more for his future success than will the best school in the land; and I would maintain this even if his training did not include the study of books.

Do not look upon the school as the legitimate agent of education for your child. Send him there by all means, if you cannot possibly teach him yourself to read and cipher. But remember that a school is at best an artificial institution, the outgrowth of the parents' proneness to relegate their highest duty to paid substitutes. The complicated machinery of the fine, large school causes you to wonder if you could possibly do anything as well as it is done there. But remember again that this grand scale of operations has been thought out for administrative purposes, not because a single educator believed children to be the gainers by being corralled into vast herds and then driven to a common goal. Just as the family is the only secure basis of the state, so is it the only safe basis of true education. If the mother will consider the many difficulties in the way of successful teaching in a large school and will then set against these in the balance the positive and unquestionable advantages of home instruction to the child she will be disposed to wonder why any child having a good home is sent to school before the age of ten. In a happy-go-lucky way we have become accustomed to think of school and study as something to which the child must inevitably proceed at the earliest possible moment. In the same measure we have lost sight of the fact that the school is burdened with parental responsibility because home training in our day is grossly neglected. Susanna Wesley taught her children at home, for twenty years carrying on this instruction daily, "not so much," she said, "to train their minds as to save their souls."

For a striking example of the effectiveness of home teaching turn to that wonderful people, the Jews, who in far-off times had no public educational system, but whose instruction was given at home by the parents. Lessons in patriotism and religion, love for the heroes of its history, enthusiasm for fellow-religionists, were given side by side with instruction from books. Here the parents projected their personality into the lives of their children. It is not strange that there is no family cohesion where the divinely ordained teachers have thrown aside their duty and farmed their children out to the school.

However, many a mother would gladly teach her children, but she distrusts her own scholarship and teaching-ability. She is rusty! She herself could not pass the examinations! They teach so differently nowadays!

The mother need not distrust her own powers nor the effectiveness of homely methods. She need not fear narrowness; it is often a blessed symptom of strength and intensity; it cuts deep instead of merely scratching the surface. Instead of worrying about methods let her gather up her courage and go ahead with this work, doing whatever seems necessary at the time, taking for guidance her own common sense and life experience, indifferent as to what particular thing the children may know, but sensitive as to what they are and can do. She will be rewarded by finding that her boys and girls at ten will know how to study, how to use a book, how to meet and overcome difficulties.

Perhaps you mothers say: That is all very fine, but we have no time to teach our children. Surely you can spare for the actual teaching one-half hour, and later one hour, each day, and that is sufficient. A child who is being taught all the time has no time to learn. It is you who know the child's mind and body. You know his prospects, needs, and possibilities. You know the importance of sincere living—of work done thoroughly and well. Above all, you will know when to let the child alone to work out its own salvation.

Moreover, whatever handicaps, real or imaginary, under which the mother teacher labors, will be more than offset by the overwhelming advantages of the simpler curriculum of her teaching, in which a pupil learns to do a few things well instead of many things poorly. Lincoln's mother, uneducated, taught her boy so effectively in the wilderness as to attain the purpose of the very best and highest teaching—which is to make a school unnecessary. Do you ask what she taught him? The alphabet, to spell, to memorize passages from the Bible, and then he learned to read the Bible. So well, indeed, did she fulfill her duty as the educator of her child that a short time ago the Chancellor of Oxford University declared to the scholars of Great Britain that among the masters of English eloquence there was not one the equal of Lincoln, the American. Such men as Franklin, Lincoln, Greeley, and many others who have acquired a high education without so-called educational advantages are generally supposed to owe their success to extraordinary powers of intellect. This in some measure may be correct. But it may be safely assumed that, driven by necessity, they studied only the subjects for which they were fit, and wasted no time on subjects for which they had neither inclination nor talent, and which, therefore, would have been useless to them.

The mother at work in her home school will become clever as she never was clever before; wiser than she could ever be for her sole self; looking so clearly into the future that you almost credit her with the gift of prophecy. She learns by teaching. Just as no amount of study or learning or experience can make an educator out of a mere instructor, so the mother's instinct, the mother's oneness with her child, the mother's patient and understanding love as she watches his growth and development will guide her to find the right way to take her all-important part in the education of her child. She needs no rigid system for teaching her children. She is not dealing with the theoretical child, but with the child as he really is.

Look at the mother hen with her brood. They obey instantly her call and her command. Let the foremost educationist of the world attempt to teach those little chicks. He meets with instant and signal defeat, and is just as likely to fail in his most persevering attempt to teach the little children of other people. The small child accepts its mother's teaching without question, even when a patient and painstaking father's instruction falls on deaf ears.

Nor need the mother attempt to teach all the subjects prescribed in the schools. It is not the acquisition, but the power of acquiring, that counts. The directness, the simplicity, the absence of showy method in home teaching help realize the dream of the educator—that to subordinate the curriculum to the good of the individual is the sound basis of education. For, while simplicity should be the watchword throughout the entire school course, the uttermost simplicity is absolutely indispensable to the effective teaching of little children, as will be attested by all who make an intelligent study of the child mind.

The young mind at first deals only with unconnected facts and single happenings. Everything is individual, standing by itself. By and by it begins combining things, seeing how two things join, discovering whereby remote and contrary things cohere, finding the relation of flower and stem. Here, then, is the first step toward complexity. Where at first the tree extended to the ground it now has roots running underground. Then comes the relationships of threes, and so on, in course of time, to the thousands. To crowd the young mind at this time with facts, to fill it with unsought information, is to preclude the natural evolution of the mental faculties by suffocating thought. For instance, the fact of the earth being round is an idea that cannot assume its full magnitude when first presented, but must have room to broaden and expand. Days and weeks and months are too short a time for the growing of this one idea. Yes, there is something on the other side of the mountain, and the earth stretches away from here to the everlasting beyond, and it doesn't just go on and on, but it doubles around until at last it comes back to this same place. And then that whole marvelous journey must be lived over again. There are seas to be crossed, and mountains to be climbed, and forests and animals and people and more mountains. A careful consideration of what a single notion such as this must mean to the little child arouses one to a sense of the danger attending the effort to teach more at one time than the child is ready to assimilate. He will ask for more information the moment he is ready for it. To teach the child all that is called for in the curriculum and claim that we are educating him is about as sensible as preparing a prize-fighter for the ring by stuffing him with all he can eat for a month beforehand.

The child unspoiled by over-instruction is as eager to learn as he is eager to play. He hungers and thirsts for knowledge. His spirit unfolds itself in questions. If we but note the scope of these questions we realize the absurdity of "fitting things to his understanding." Here is a soul hungering for its proper food. He wants to know the biggest things in creation. Who is really equal, who can be equal, to answering the questions of a little child? Instead of planning set lessons that you think suited to his understanding, if you could only yield wisely and let yourself follow the lead of the child, teaching him what he will insist upon knowing, you would want no other pedagogy. "A little child shall lead them." This can truly apply to the intellectual training of the child. It can well be the mother's guide in choosing what is to be taught, and when. Just as the tendrils of the vine reach out for something solid, so the growing mind of the child is putting forth questions, seeking something sure to which it may cling. Its questions are parts of an uncompleted whole in his experience. They and their satisfying answers are the warp and woof of its intellectual growth. *The time to teach him a thing is the moment he shows you his mind is ready for that thing.* Here you have the psychological moment talked about so much, but of which we cannot take advantage in the graded school.

All of childhood is a schooling, and the child in his first six years learns relatively more than he will learn hereafter in his entire school course. Is not the relative distance between the infant and the child of six greater than the relative distance between the latter and the university graduate? The training of the body comes before the training of the mind, as every mother realizes, and the formation of right habits precedes in time and importance instruction from books. Indeed, all artificial lessons, all work with books, may be long delayed, months and years being spent in getting ready for their use. The time to begin the study of books will vary so much with the individual that no hard and fast general law can be given. In later chapters are given unpretentious methods of teaching various subjects, but they are only intended to be suggestive. The entire plan of work given in this book is based upon the assumption that your five-year-old is being trained in habits of orderliness and regularity, helpfulness and unquestioning obedience. These are plain, true aims of education, the ones most often overlooked. Such training as this is the highest kind of discipline, forming habits of immeasurable worth. To give this kind of training the earnest mother cannot doubt her ability. Even if difficult in the beginning, its value is supreme and makes easy and delightful the later task of educating the child.

It may appear unfair to propose an added responsibility in the case of the mother who must do her housework without help or with but one servant, but in reality such conditions are most favorable to the education of the child.

The best teaching I ever saw in my life was done by the busy mother of nine children, who taught her little ones as she worked about the house. She would give the little girl a handful of beans to count, then to find half of them. Perhaps the child would divide the beans equally among her family of clothes-pin dolls and see how many fell to the share of each. The recitation took place during the daily combing of the child's tangled curls. Fortunately for this small girl, she lived far back in the wilderness, miles from a schoolhouse, and after learning to read and getting the elements of arithmetic, she pursued the study of mathematics at home. Sometimes she asked her mother for aid, and it came in this form: "I shall certainly help you if you want me to, but remember that every time you get a hard example by your own effort it is worth twenty that I help you with." The child would turn to her book with renewed courage and struggle on at the stubborn problem. Again would she appeal for help, and this time it would be: "Read the first part of the problem carefully until you are sure you understand it. You can get the meaning of the first sentence?" Yes, the child could. "Now study the next part of it—no more—until you know what that means. Then see if these two sentences are clear to you." Over and over the small child would study the problem in this way, whether it was arithmetic or algebra. She actually mastered these subjects with the aid of her mother, who had never opened an algebra in her life, but who did know how a child should study.

Teach these essentials: How to work; that "Heaven is not reached at a single bound;" that habits early formed determine character and destiny; that "genius is an infinite capacity for taking pains;" that "He that ruleth his own spirit is greater than he that taketh a city;" that tomorrow will soon be yesterday; that we must make our opportunities, not wait for them; that all work is ennobling, idleness unfruitful, degrading, abhorrent to God and man.

At what age, then, should these essentials be acquired? They should unquestionably be mastered before the age of ten. The right foundation cannot be more dispensed with in an education than in a structure of brick and stone. The latter is but temporal, while in the former we are building for eternity. Discipline of mind and character is a first object; all else is secondary to character-building. In these very early years is laid the foundation of character; if the plan be faulty, the workmen unskilled, the material second rate, then all later acquisitions of knowledge based upon this are building for naught. We have a house built upon sand.

Our aim from beginning to end shall be power-getting, making each year really represent a year's preparation for life, instead of being merely a preparation for the succeeding grade. To this end we shall eliminate unnecessary and worthless branches by applying to every subject, and to each detail of every subject, the test:

Is this worth learning?
Does this particular child need it?

Is this the time to teach it?
Is it something he will be able to master of his own accord later on?

Then let the teacher apply to her own work the further test: Let me teach this day as if it were the last day to be vouchsafed me for my work.

The child is to acquire interest and ambition, the desire to learn, habits of industry and perseverance. I do not think we should try to make things too easy for stout boys and girls, nor have them learn things with the least possible exertion. We must convince them that nothing worth while has ever been done except by persistent, unremitting effort.

We shall endeavor to bring the current of education within narrow bounds, to make it deep and strong and swift-flowing, instead of dissipating its power and destroying its usefulness by spreading it over vast areas.

What becomes of the little child while the mother is doing her housework? The child will be taught and made to help, and so will be getting the best of teaching. At ten years of age every boy and girl should be able to help intelligently with every task about the house, garden, and farm. In the beginning let him help in the kitchen drying the knives and forks, placing the dishes carefully away. With a tiny broom he can sweep the kitchen. He can help with the bed-making. With a cloth he can carefully dust pieces of furniture, the chairs, the sewing-machine. Thus, safe under his mother's eye, happy in his activity, asking questions, learning good and helpful lessons, the day passes. Something of a hindrance to his mother, perhaps, but a loving hindrance; and becoming less of a hindrance as he learns to be more and more useful. He takes your time and attention. But is not the welfare of a human soul more important than the matter of a dessert for dinner?

Another ready solution of the problem of primary instruction is the neighborhood school. In nearly every community is some mother, perhaps herself a former teacher, who can help her less experienced neighbors by gathering their little ones in with her own children and thus conducting a school of individual instruction.

Not only does such a school meet the real needs of its own pupils, especially such as have no playmates at home, but it affords a point of leverage for the reform of the public school. For we "must cry aloud and spare not." Said a well-known school-director in whose home such a neighborhood school has been carried on: "If it were a matter of instructing my own children exclusively, I would not send them to any other school; but what about those with whom my children will associate and whom they will marry when they grow up? I must better their conditions, which means I must wrestle with the public-school problem; hence my determination to work for the reform of the public school."

Such a neighborhood school as I am advocating should be small, consisting of from six to ten pupils, with a course of study and a school-day planned to fit the needs of these children. The teacher will not concern herself with the manner in which some one else would carry on a school. She is unhampered by tradition, or system, or supervision. She is bound by no rules save those of common sense; she has only to consider her duty to God and the parents.

She pins her faith to simple, honest, everyday work. She will insist upon a day's work that is just a little better, higher, more complete than that of the day before. A piece of work is well done or it is not well done. Instead of hearing recitations she will spend the time in directing the children's work. She will not waste time on averages or examinations.

Such a school as this, carried on for the love of the work by a competent, earnest teacher with pupils who have never known artificial stimuli to interest, is worth much in this age of superficiality. Here every child will be taught to work to the best advantage according to the inherent capacity of each, and neither excuse nor substitute will be accepted for an honest day's work. They will be taught how to study. They will be made to realize the value of time.

Energy will be devoted to mind-training instead of mind-cramming. The mere acquisition of knowledge is a minor concern.

The whole environment will be conducive to study. There is an atmosphere of work. When the teacher is left free to exercise her faculties in the planning of work you may hope for inspiration to flow outward to the children. The careful employment of any faculty means the intensifying and developing of that faculty to the worker.

As a last word let me say, Keep your child out of bad company, at home and at school. "He that toucheth pitch will be defiled." The home is responsible for the moral and religious training of the child. Religious education in the schools is and ever will be a vexing question; it must make no distinction; it must be only such teaching as is embodied in the cardinal virtues, in Pope's "Universal Prayer," in "Lead, Kindly Light," and must not in any sense be sectarian, for the experience of ages in many lands has shown that the results of mixing sectarian with general education have been as disastrous as those of combining religion and politics. Voltaire, Gibbon, and Ingersoll were all "religiously educated," and lived to be the enemies of all religion. On the other hand, from the earliest years the child must have religious training imparted by father and mother with all the earnestness of deep sincerity. Childhood is the time to instill matters of faith, nor is it in the order of nature to hope that, neglected in early years, it may be implanted later on or that it will come as a matter of reason. The home training makes possible the use of chosen parts of the Bible as a text-book, the reading and memorizing of which has been a part of the early training of great men of diverse creeds and talents. Indeed, the first chapter of Genesis has furnished the material for spelling, reading, and memorizing, as taught by the mother of many a great man.

V

POETRY, A POTENT EDUCATIONAL FACTOR

POETRY, the natural language of mankind, can be made a potent educational factor. In the early stages of civilization peoples possessing neither models nor instruction, created poetry which our highest civilization can only feebly imitate. Whether we turn to the Old Testament, to the early literature of Greece and Rome, to that of ancient Wales and Brittany, or to the Arthurian and Nibelungen legends, we find spontaneous poetry and its materials such as our denaturalized culture refuses longer to yield. Modern poetry, like modern life, is too complex to be acceptable to the unsophisticated mind. In the old Gaelic literature there are legends resplendent with a beauty pertaining to altogether new things. The child also is looking upon a world crowded with marvelous new things. Early poetry, therefore, or that dealing with primitive things, is especially attuned to the child mind.

Poetry does not mean merely rhythmical verses and jingling rhymes that please by their meter and similarity of terminal or initial sounds. Poetry is the expression of beautiful thought in harmonious language. It is art and thought in one. It marks the middle ground between the thought and the thing, between man and nature, where feeling glides into reasoning. Poetry interprets life for us. Primitive poetry is based upon specific concerns intimately related to man — singleness of ideas, of action, of purpose. When the world was young gods walked the earth and mingled with men. The great poems arise with the traditional folk-tales. Such poems as the "Iliad" and the "Odyssey," which were the delight of infant Greece, were handed down by word of mouth through many generations.

Poetry is inborn in man; it is the language of childhood. So the child, with an inventive fancy that enriches everything, may be called a poet. Stevenson says every boy is "part poet, part pirate, part pig." He has within him latent forces, possibilities of immeasurable extent, the traits and tendencies of a hundred ancestors, a mind so plastic that every touch makes an indelible mark. He participates in the eternal. Yet he thinks in terms of his own experience, and asks: Is God everywhere? Is He in the garden? Then if I throw a stone, do I hit God? Does He own everything? Does He own my toys? Isn't God selfish if He owns my toys? Each child is to itself the center of a world bounded by the horizon of its experiences and peopled largely by the creations of its mind. For the child time, space, and number have no meaning. The world is full of beauty, and the child is full of awe. No long use has dimmed the eye of the young soul. The commonplace is wonderful, and the wonderful and terrible are commonplace. The most common objects are glorified. The meadow brook is a mighty stream. The rose-bush towers above his head. There is no definite line between the real and the unreal. The little fellow longs to follow the woodland path for a glimpse of the giant castle in the forest gloom. He dreams of the marvelous land the mountain hides from view. Even the *Tales of the Arabian Nights* might easily have been enacted in his own back yard. The splendor of their imagery and their wealth of exaggeration do not strike inharmoniously the powerful fancy of the child, with its wistful, longing, colorful dreams.

He who knows the mind of the child, knows the evolution of the mind of the race, and understands the well-established truth that the history of the individual epitomizes the history of mankind. The ancient sagas, with their figurative and heroic language, reflect the characteristics of the early peoples—their intensity of feeling, their facts and fancies, their strength and weaknesses—all mental characteristics of the little child. And just as the race grew out of the age of poetry into the age of reasoning, so is it with the child. From the age of poetry we pass on to that of prose and reason. Reason and logic, unlike poetry, are subject to the active control of the mature mind only.

The love of poetry is never a product of reasoning. It springs from and is cultivated through the feelings. It is a matter of faith. It requires the believing frame of mind characteristic of the infancy of the world. Childhood is the time of faith. The young child is naturally a poet. It may be said that at the age of about ten the child is prepared to emerge from the region of fancy, the riot of imagination, the society of the poet and the dreamer, from fairyland, to the sobering prose of fact. Reasoning manifests itself; imagination loosens its tenacious hold; judgments, even if intemperate, begin to be formed. Now the language of prose begins to find a place, not at first superseding entirely the thought and diction of the poet, but running side by side there-with, and at no time without interwoven threads. As the reasoning faculties develop and the critical talents grow keener the children become cynical, and begin to feel ashamed of their old poetical ardor. Therefore let us give the child real poetry during the years when his imagination is receptive for the thought of the poet, for by delay the gift is lost. This endowment should be nourished with care. That is a ghastly literary training that does not feed the heart and imagination. To deprive the young child of poetry is to starve a soul hungering for its proper food.

In its early years, then, the child ought to study the best poems in our language, and memorize some of the masterpieces. The reading should consist chiefly of real poetry, not merely of good verse. Better than at any subsequent period, you can thus form the child's literary taste. It is not necessary to make him acquainted with all or even many of the masterpieces. Here the saying of the old Greek holds good, that the half is often more than the whole. A single poem carefully studied, memorized, and loved will do more for the child than a dozen that are indifferently skimmed. The trouble is that real poetry is too often left until late in the course of instruction, while trash, supposed to fit the child's intellect, is substituted. This is absurd and harmful. If we nurture the minds of our children during the early years on the best literature, if we place them in the society of great men, they will not be satisfied with the dime novel or the "best-seller" in later years.

Many a teacher will be appalled at the idea of presenting Mark Antony's speech to boys and girls of nine years. Why not give it to them? The language itself is not too difficult. True, some of the thought is above their appreciation, as it often is above the adult's. Were it not so, it would not be worth reading. You do not expect to get from any fine piece the whole significance at first, but only after exhaustive study and familiarity. Not only ought the child to read Mark Antony's speech and feel and enjoy it, but he should memorize every word. He will never tire of repeating the phrases, for each new time he finds something in them that he had not felt before. Tell the children of Julius Caesar, the man, in such a way that not a child in the room will be indifferent. This done, we need not fear but that some day they will read Roman history without compulsion. We are not striving to produce prodigies, but we surely want the children to carry something of culture and taste into their everyday life. It would be hard to form a series of lessons richer in literary content, and more potent to cultivate simple, energetic, picturesque expression than this speech. The very words are animate with spirit. Heart and mind alike are stirred, and the child's appreciation of its power, beauty, and simplicity will increase as the years go by. One of the reasons for selecting this piece of poetry is that it is one of the few things that will never grow stale with use. It will live through the ages. The child will love it as soon as he can understand it, and the man of seventy will love it still more.

Some may protest that this or an equally good poem is too long to be memorized by young children. We shall not ask them to learn it all in one day or in a week, but any child can commit to memory four or five lines at a lesson. Assign a suitable portion to be first LEARNED and then written correctly from memory. When completed the whole poem should be written from beginning to end without consulting a guide. This is a real test of ability.

We can introduce even five-year-olds to great and sublime poems. It should not be necessary to justify our pleading by saying that the best in literature is not too good for the youngest children. We should not have had to do so fifty and more years ago. But modern methods and the routine of our schools keep the child from early acquaintance with masterpieces. Why not choose the best poetry instead of the regulation stock of First Readers and Supplementary Readers? We should not longer waste the child's most impressionable period upon the unlovely, the absurd, or the commonplace. Perhaps you recall how the cat sat on the mat and chased the rat; how the frog sat on the log and sang; the ox ate out of the box; the dog bit the cow's tail. Would you not prefer that so much effort of your own had been expended in storing your mind with the magnificent, subtle, and picturesque ideas embodied in the noblest literature? The irresistible power of great writers impels their devotees to seek these things not only in literature, but in all life.

In the schools of the past the memory was cultivated beyond the other faculties, and sometimes, it might appear, to the exclusion of the others. Yet this was not entirely bad, for at least the mind had in itself the material upon which the other faculties, such as imagination, feeling, and emotion, could thrive. The individual had knowledge as a foundation for thinking, and whether he learned to think or not depended a good deal upon the man himself.

To-day the memory is neglected. This may sound extreme to people who have heard much said of the cramming in our schools, the memorizing of definitions, and the gorging for examinations. But such things consist, in the main, of isolated, scrappy information, bits of knowledge having little permanent value, taken into the mind with the understanding that it is to be retained but temporarily. Reason says to Memory: "Just hang on to this for a little while, until that test is passed, and then let it go." Excessive reading weakens the memory. Quite different indeed was the practice of learning long and difficult poems, whole chapters from the Bible, speeches of the world's great orators, books of the Iliad and Odyssey—things that have literary content, fine pictures for the mind's gallery, and lessons for life. If equal in the first place to the strain of acquiring, the mind fed upon such things as these becomes strengthened. Let us have today more of the things that feed the imagination in a healthful way, for one of the greatest things in the world is imagination.

Every little child should learn the Mother Goose rhymes. They are based, though perhaps unconsciously, upon psychological principles, in that they tell stories within the comprehension of universal childhood, and tell them in the order in which the equivalent questions arise in the child's mind. The following scheme, showing the natural sequence of the story in Mother Goose rhymes, was discovered by an ingenious mother in telling the rhyme to her little boy. She began with the line, "A little boy went into the barn," then paused, waiting for a very natural question. It came shortly, "Then what did he do?" Mother Goose answers, "He lay down in the hay." After a moment of thought came the next question, "And then what happened?" And again Mother Goose answers, "An owl came out and flew about." From the time the child can speak give him Mother Goose. Did you ever realize the very important part that is played in literature by such characters as Old King Cole or Tweedledum and Tweedledee?

These rhymes belong to the kindergarten period. Having passed that, the child can begin to learn the beautiful epic "Hiawatha." You will be told by popular writers and lecturers that the children love the poems written by the children's poets, such as Stevenson and Eugene Field. These two men and others have indeed written exquisite poems of childhood, but it is you and I that enjoy them, not the children, while "Hiawatha," though not written primarily for children, is the child's poem. Children, given their choice between "The Duel," by Field, or "My Shadow," by Stevenson, on the one hand, and either a repetition or a continuation of "Hiawatha" on the other, will seldom make the latter take second place.

There is no reason why every American child is not better and happier for knowing by heart the folk-epic of his land. It is so constructed that the difficulties gradually but materially increase, keeping pace with the learner's increasing powers, and with the growth and learning of the hero. Because of this continuity of thought and structure its educational value is incomparably greater than an equal QUANTITY of good but assorted literature. One of the faults of the public schools is the fragmentary teaching that precludes any systematic study. A single great poem learned and loved is worth a smattering of a hundred.

If the mother is not on friendly terms with this poem she will be repaid for cultivating familiarity with it, reading the whole and acquiring the pronunciation of the Indian names. Then, too, there is a real advantage in memorizing beforehand the lines she will give the child for a lesson. She repeats these lines many times and lets the learner say them with her. She may do this day after day and the child will not weary of it. You are taking advantage of that stage in its mental development when it rejoices in repetition, demanding a favorite story over and over, the details of which must not vary one jot nor tittle. The child will learn a few new lines each week, but the time element matters little. You are giving him this beautiful creation, a new world; you are making him appreciate a great poem, and you are doing no small thing.

Some may object: "How can a child learn a poem which it cannot read?" Teach the poem little by little, just as Mother Goose was given. Begin with these resonant lines:

> By the shores of Gitche Gumee,
> By the shining Big-Sea-Water,
> Stood the wigwam of Nokomis,
> Daughter of the Moon, Nokomis.
> Dark behind it rose the forest,
> Rose the black and gloomy pine-trees,
> Rose the firs with cones upon them.

The child must see the lake, the Gitche Gumee, the Big-Sea-Water. And if in his horizon there is no shining Big-Sea-Water, no firs with cones upon them, you certainly can get pictures of them. Here are new words of the every-day kind—SHORES, FOREST—which are to be made clear. The boy or girl will listen to these lines many times and will repeat them over and over, with the following to complete the picture:

Bright before it beat the water,
Beat the clear and sunny water,
Beat the shining Big-Sea-Water.

Words are things. That word FOREST perhaps opens up new possibilities of thought and fancy to the child. Consider the words and phrases these few lines have added to his vocabulary — not isolated words, but used in a proper setting where each speaks forth its meaning: *shores, forest, gloomy, pine-trees, upon them, behind it, before it, beat, sunny water*. Few stronger arguments for the teaching of real poetry need be advanced than this widening of the vocabulary in the direction of plain, simple speech. The words so strung together secure to themselves a permanency in the mind. Beside verses such as these, the much-favored infant food, "I Love little Pussy, Her coat is so warm," and kindred compositions, seem no more soul-satisfying than the dancing of a wooden doll.

The true epic marshals for us the scenes and thoughts in orderly array, as just shown—first the landscape, then we are introduced to the young hero:

There the wrinkled old Nokomis
Nursed the little Hiawatha,
Rocked him in his linden cradle,
Bedded soft in moss and rushes,
Safely bound with reindeer sinews;
Stilled his fretful wail by saying,
"Hush! the Naked Bear will hear thee!"
Lulled him into slumber, singing,
"Ewa-yea! my little owlet!

Who is this, that lights the wigwam?
With his great eyes lights the wigwam?
Ewa-yea! my little owlet!"

In these twelve lines will be found many allusions that must be made clear—stories of Indian children, descriptions of the reindeer, home life of the owl and owlet. Answer the child's questions, but do not spoil the whole undertaking by questioning him at every point nor by thrusting explanations upon him. Once, when a small learner failed to ask the meaning of "fretful wail," the writer was betrayed by curiosity into asking if he knew what the words meant. Immediately by way of definition came forth a realistic imitation of the wail of a fretful baby.

The poem should be read with expression again and again, so that the pictures are clear, the ideas associated, the rhythm felt. Memorizing will then very nearly take care of itself. But as it is not alone the pictures and the idea we want, but the rhythm as well, the child must learn the words exactly right, so that he will not make the blunder later on, as many grown people do, of shortening or lengthening the quoted line, as though a syllable more or less did not make much difference. Frequently you will hear even a good teacher, in attempting to repeat from memory such a line as, "Saw the moon rise from the water," say inadvertently, "Saw the *great* moon rise from the water," thus utterly destroying the meter, a thing she would not have done in any selection had she really learned poetry in childhood.

Now consider the passage immediately following:

Many things Nokomis taught him.

In these lines you have the opportunity of bringing to the beginner a glimpse of surrounding worlds—the stars, the comet, the Northern Lights, the Milky Way. These will furnish material for many an engrossing talk. Next comes a part of the poem filled with music, poetry, nature, life. It sings itself to the heart of the child from first to last.

> At the door on summer evenings
> Sat the little Hiawatha.

And the lines following.

The child who has learned by heart the first fifty lines of Hiawatha's childhood wants to know what the little Indian boy did next. He is filled with the mysterious charm of the poem, and does not want to leave this little Indian, now his friend and spirit playmate. He wants to hear more of his experiences, real events, for nothing is more genuine to a child than the things of the imagination. He learns the meaning of the words as he goes along, and the mother will have her hands full explaining these definitions. Take just one part of the poem at a time, such as the story of the moon, story of the rainbow, the owls hooting in the forest. With each advanced part you will notice that the child memorizes with greater ease, and you can proceed to the teaching of English.

VI

HOW TO TEACH ENGLISH

WHAT are the first steps in teaching a child to read "Hiawatha" and other poems for itself? The method is dictated by unbiased common sense. Start in as your mother was taught, and as she would have taught you. Begin with the alphabet in the old-fashioned way. Teach the names of the letters. The letter is "S," not "the sound the snake makes when it is angry." Again, it is "M," not "the sound the bossy cow makes." Give the child credit for having intelligence. In the first place you yourself are not much interested in a thing whose name you do not know. A child does not ask "What is that for?" nor "What does it do?" He asks, "What is that?" meaning its name. Would you refuse to tell a child, "That is a fence," but explain its nature as "a barrier to ingress and egress"? For learning the alphabet no text-book is needed. The child may learn the alphabet from its blocks, which are a most effective medium. Show the letter A, and ask the beginner to see how many of these it can find. Let the boy or girl make the letters by laying sticks. With blunt scissors he or she may cut out the letters from old papers. All this is training the eye, the judgment, the awkward little fingers. Devise games with the letters to teach spelling, and gradually and slowly teach the sounds represented by the letters.

When the child has learned a considerable amount of poetry and knows the alphabet and something of spelling and phonetics, it may be given a book. It associates and connects the memorized words with their printed symbols. Suddenly it makes the discovery that the printed page holds something of boundless interest. It has been acquiring a love of poetry which is only cultivated through the feelings. It brings to the words glowing thought and reads into them a life and vitality such as the historic rat and cat never inspired.

As for the child being already familiar with what he is to read, it is true here, as elsewhere, that you get out of a book, a sermon, a college course, what you bring to it. "He that would bring home the wealth of the Indies must carry out the wealth of the Indies." Only the thinking mind gets new thoughts from the printed page. When the mind is braced with ideas, with self-relying thought, then the pages of whatever book we read become luminous with manifold allusion. In the public school the child acquires a mechanical aptitude for pronouncing the symbols for words, and then the name of reading is applied to the result. The pronunciation of the word, the phrase, the sentence, may be perfect; the understanding of what is read is nil. Reading is of less importance than mind-training, so let the child memorize long selections before asking him to read. It is not time lost. Then without ceremony give him the book. At the first line, "By the shores of Gitche Gumee," he may begin to spell out the words. Considering that he knows this by heart, he will not have to spell many of them for you. How often a little child says, "Please let me alone; I can read this by myself." Do not hurry him by helping him unsolicited. This discovery of his that he can read is one of the important moments of his life.

You may ask why the reading offered for the second or a later year is of the same kind as that for the first. Although the same material is given to all children to read, to memorize, and to spell, no hard and fast rule as to quantity is laid down, except that each shall strike his own gait, shall ask his own questions, shall take his own time to learn. A list of questions to develop the subject is not furnished in this book. That is left to the child and the poet. They have always been rare company for each other.

Our reading-lesson might occasionally be conducted after this fashion. Let us suppose that the children have learned the alphabet and can spell a few words. Write on the board the lines:

At the door on summer evenings
Sat the little Hiawatha.

Perhaps the children have already memorized this. They may read it. They may copy it. More of the passage will be read, discussed, memorized, written on the board. The mother may illustrate it. Answer the children's questions. Such a lesson as this will doubtless fill the entire period in the home school, but in it we have taught all the essentials except arithmetic. We have taught reading, writing, drawing, geography, history; we have been training the eye, the ear, the hand, we have fed the imagination and developed the memory. We may do more than this. The teacher's drawings on the board in colored crayon will be a source of delight and inspiration to the little ones, who will eagerly imitate them. There may be one child whose special gift is in this direction, and he will not be satisfied with merely copying, but will make his drawing express his own interpretation of the poem. By all means encourage this. We ought to watch always for indications of the child's special gift, and when we find talent we should foster it. Take the seemingly stupid boy and find out his difficulty. You may be rewarded by discovering that his mind is busy with things far beyond his years. The test of a good school is the facility with which its scheme adapts itself to every human intellect.

The work may profitably begin at a regular time each day. Do not stop a child who is working earnestly at one thing in order to have him do something else. This is the way teachers destroy concentration, the lack of which they afterward bewail. It matters little what kind of activity is employed, if the child is busy of his own volition; it means growth and unfolding. It cannot be too often said that much of the success of this teaching depends upon doing one thing only at a time and doing it thoroughly. Do not undertake several subjects in a day, each for a few minutes, but have steady, persistent work upon one until something real is accomplished.

Stories are a necessary part of child life. *Æsop's Fables* seem the very primer of worldly wisdom, teaching good lessons for life. What greater fun is there for a little fellow than to take his box of letters and spell out the story of the Fox and the Grapes, either with your help or copying it from the book? Then leave the story on the table for father's admiration when he comes home from work. Use these stories, too, for training in close attention. Tell one of them to the child and let him repeat it to you. Do this every day. Before many days the stories may substantially increase in length. This practice teaches a child to express himself coherently and to better advantage than will a later course in rhetoric. Naturally we should choose stories that the child likes, but at the same time our serious purpose is to produce a taste for sober reading. Do not imagine that the two aims are incompatible. There are stories that lead to the enjoyment of the Bible and of Shakespeare, even of the essayists. So read your boy the poems that he likes, the fairy stories and the fables and legends that never grow old. They will all expand his mind. In another place is given a list of the poems that may profitably be known by the time a child is eight or nine. A few of the good books the mother can read aloud are also listed. Some will say these selections are too hard for the child, but we are not looking for easy things. The reading that is hard for a child is the reading out of which he gets something. Of course there are numberless books that an eight-year-old would be able to read and may want to read, but if it has only a few books much is made of that few. It is not a good thing for a child to be humped over a book all day. Bodily activity comes first. Like other young animals, children need it. A child of six or seven should be working with the mother about the house helping with the different tasks, and in this way learning to do them. Besides helping, he ought to play with other children, and also to play alone for a while. Since he is learning in every waking moment, more than all else he should have plenty of sleep.

As a typical result of the early training of the mind through reading, the following example by an experimental school may be offered. Some pupils who had entered after two years in a public high school were told to memorize Bryant's "Thanatopsis." Every member of the class protested that this was an impossibility—no one ever did such a thing. Then a class of children about twelve years old, who had had two years of good training, were assigned the same task. They fell to work, and in a few days succeeded. A child of nine, whose whole teaching had been individual, asked permission to learn the assignment. Under other circumstances this piece of literature would not have been given to one so young. But in this case she was told that she might learn the poem. She mastered it, including spelling and definitions of terms, in half the time of the children of twelve who had a different foundation, and they in turn mastered it in half the time of the pupils of seventeen, who had been shamed into an honest effort to get the lesson.

There is another type of English work which will necessitate more of the mother's time than that so far discussed, but it will satisfy the needs of the child, so the mother will feel repaid. Let the mother take Longfellow's "Courtship of Miles Standish," and study the poem carefully, looking up in the dictionary the words that are no longer in daily use. Let her refresh her memory with a little historical research; then when well armed begin to read this poem to the little learner. The first four lines are given as an illustration :

> In the old Colony days, in Plymouth the land of the Pilgrims,
> To and fro in a room of his simple and primitive dwelling,
> Clad in doublet and hose, and boots of Cordovan leather.
> Strode, with a martial air, Miles Standish the Puritan captain.

Pedagogically, you are supposed to deal with the complete sentence, but how can you do it here? We shall not try. You can only go as far as "In the old Colony days." You will have questions aplenty to answer. It will probably be the afternoon of the next day before you get the chance to complete the line and make mention of Plymouth the land of the Pilgrims. What was Plymouth? And who were the Pilgrims? There is no use thinking you can go further until this is threshed out. What? Take two days to read one line of poetry?

Our reading is not to be pronouncing words, but thought-getting. You will not get far in this before you have satisfied yourself of the educative value of "answering the child's questions." Now when the first line is plain sailing read it again, with the next. Do not explain "to and fro" unless you are asked. See if the meaning cannot be suggested by the context. Have you never visited a school-room and wished you could muzzle the talkative teacher who gave the children no time to think? But the primitive dwelling, the log cabin of the settler, you must be prepared to describe minutely in word and picture. And you must be just as ready to present the doughty little warrior, his doublet and hose and leather boots. Then read these four lines, for the rhythm as much as for the vocabulary. Here and there ask the child to repeat the passage after you, but do not stipulate that he give it in the words of the book, nor in his own words; in fact, say nothing as to the manner of presentation, but let it truly be given in the child's own way.

This suggestion will indicate the treatment of the whole poem. But remember it is not adapted to all children of seven or even eight, and it is one of the things not to be given if the child does not want it. Just think of what this treatment of the entire poem would embody: learning new words, within the child's comprehension, yet difficult, and so giving him a superior vocabulary; training his ear to a sense of rhythm; adding bountifully to his stock of information. Here is history and geography taught in the natural way, and it might be added that it is as near the formal teaching of these subjects as is desirable before the tenth year. Another valuable feature of this long poem is that the interest will be great enough to carry the child to the completion of the work. Through this sustained interest and attention we develop voluntary concentration.

When this stage of progress has been reached more heed may be given to written English, but there need be only the simplest principles of technical grammar. The study of grammar has little to do with correctness of speech or writing; these depend more upon home training. Technical grammar is excellent mind-training for the right period, as are mathematics, but that period does not begin during the first ten years of the child's life. We should have written reproductions of such models as "The Legend of Sleepy Hollow" and "Evangeline," letter-writing, and much copying of the best poetry and prose. Few realize the wonderful benefit to be obtained from copying for a half-hour daily the best passages from our great authors. Copying good literature obviates the need of memorizing rules for punctuation and capital letters. In no other way can a degree of scholastic ability be attained so surely. Reading is indeed good, but transcribing has immeasurably greater value. To form the habit in childhood of giving a period of intensive study daily to the great masters of our language constitutes a training that indescribably furthers the pursuit of scholarship. Looking up the definition of each word that is new, rare, interesting, or difficult gives a richness of vocabulary that is a fair index of richness of thought. Perhaps it is to this kind of study that Emerson refers when he says that one hour spent in study each day will make of an ignorant man a well-informed one in ten years.

A well-known writer was recently asked how she had obtained her education, and, particularly, her expressive and picturesque vocabulary, that seems to have a flavor other than that of the schools. With her permission the story is reproduced here:

"As a small child I was eager to read, and seeing my father sit night after night with a volume of poetry in his hand, plainly enjoying the contents, I would seek the same book by day, vainly trying to understand and enjoy it also. I complained to my mother that the book did not say anything, so mother told me to read the same selection a great many times and it would say something. This I did, having chanced upon Longfellow's "Sands of the Desert in an Hour-Glass" until much of the meaning became clear to me. Other single poems became intelligible and a delight by the same method. As this occurred when I was eight years old, you will see that it is not an example of precocity. I grew to like poetry, reading the same things many, many times, finding something new at each reading. A year later I was presented with a volume, Lytton's *Kenelm Chillingly*, whose pompous English style had proved insufferably heavy for the former owner. Though now an omnivorous reader and a lover of the very feel of a book, I looked into my treasure with some dismay, of how could any one make sense out of those monstrous words? Yet a sense of loyalty to the donor or of shame at acknowledging my distress, incited me to diligence. So I opened the book and the dictionary side by side and went to work. Nor did the proceeding prove distasteful. The reading at first went very slowly, since so many new words must be defined, but by and by I noticed that in looking for one word other meanings and words were noted, that I was later to meet, and the sense of growing power decreased the labor and brightened the task, so that the completion of the book marked a distinct epoch in my life. At nine I had learned how to study and had formed the study habit, had developed concentration and perseverance to an important and noticeable degree, and had acquired the power to do a piece of hard work.

"The next year came another phase of my education. Thackeray's *Vanity Fair* fell into my hands, and I abandoned myself to the joy of that wonderful book. Understand it? No, only here and there. But scarcely had I begun when my older brother, whom I worshiped, eyed the title with disapproval and suggested that I should not waste my time on novels—I might better be studying. Here was certainly a crisis. I would not for ten thousand worlds displease that brother by ignoring his advice, nor could I possibly relinquish the book. My mind suggested a compromise. I would copy the book as I went along, for surely copying was disagreeable enough to be called studying. This satisfied my brother, and that entire volume was written painstakingly in what was at first a featureless scrawl, and at last the characteristic hand of to-day.

"In this undertaking I discovered certain fixed usages pertaining to punctuation and such points that had not attracted attention when I merely read *Kenelm Chillingly* with my friend, the dictionary. The use of commas seemed to be governed by certain laws that

I came to recognize long before I could put them into words. Semicolons, too, had a nice way of balancing a sentence, although at times I could not satisfy myself that a period would not have done just as well. Capitals were easily accounted for, and I personally liked the paragraphs for the way in which they were indented. All of these points I carefully reproduced in my manuscript."

"In time I came too observe something of the laws of structure, that related sentences were grouped into a paragraph, that a new chapter usually dealt with new incidents or scenes, and that the book did not tell you at the beginning the important thing it had to say, but led you carefully to it. This was the way in which I learned to write."

The method so indicated is simple, yet most effective; it is hard, yet not too difficult. It is not a new scheme of education, and would pass unquestioned by such men as Franklin or Horace Greeley.

Here is an English lesson planned to occupy our entire school. Read a selection to the children—a page or less. Going back to the first, I reread a passage and ask for this to be told to me. Every one sets to thinking, and when I get a good, clear-cut sentence I write it on the board. If no sentence good enough is offered, I give one. I continue in this way for perhaps half an hour, during which time I have held the interest of all, for all have an equal chance of giving an acceptable answer, and I have a creditable paragraph or more on the board. Then the children copy this. The little ones get a few words written, the older ones the whole exercise, and the advanced students are permitted to continue in their own way, telling the passage read. Thus an hour, often more, gives one the best effort of every child in the room.

Little ones love repetition. We should take advantage of this by letting them have the good poems over and over. I taught Mark Antony's speech to some children of seven. They memorized the whole of it in about six weeks. Yet there was scarcely a day throughout the remainder of the year that these children did not come to me and ask me to read them this poem. They knew it by heart, yet they would rather listen to it than go out to play.

This brings us again to the subject of reading. Learning to read must go hand in hand with the taste for the worth-while in reading, else you will agree with me that the individual is better off, and the world better off, for his not learning to read. I defy any one to show me that reading in itself has served one good turn for people whose sole literature is the daily paper and the vicious novel.

Let us recapitulate.

Reading should be the great essential in the instruction of a child.

The right way is indicated in this chapter on teaching English.

Follow the wrong way, and trouble begins with the beginning.

Hothouse methods of teaching this subject are responsible for the chief difficulty in the public-school course.

The so-called sight method goes to create superficiality because the child calls a word what it looks like, not what it is. This habit, then, permeates all his work. It is an artificial method. Rapid pronunciation of words is called reading. The aim is rapidity instead of thoroughness.

The meaning of word or passage or selection is not to be taken into account. The reading does not need to mean anything. Therefore it is not reading.

Much more is attempted than can possibly be carried out, ever so much more than in the schools of olden times.

Showy and artificial methods have crowded out and usurped the place of plain, natural methods.

The aim is quantity, not quality.

An essential subject is so crowded with worthless detail as to obscure real worth and make discrimination difficult.

VII

HOW TO TEACH SPELLING

IT needs but little argument to convince an interested mother that her child should be a good speller. If reading is the main tool of knowledge-getting, then spelling is assuredly the first requisite of good reading. To be a good speller implies more than the mere ability to avoid errors in orthography and so to win approbation for mechanical nicety. A habit of accuracy and consistency, though it be only in the writing of words, may well lead toward forming like habits in deeds.

We learn to spell only by spelling. The "improved" methods of teaching reading ignore to an alarming extent the place and value of spelling in school and in life. They treat the word as a whole to be recognized by sight, and train the child to call a word, not what it is, but what it looks to be. The real way to know a word is to be acquainted with its parts. As some discussion is given to this in the chapter on English, from the point of view of learning to read, we shall be brief here.

Many a mother fears to teach her child to spell lest it interfere with his fitting nicely into the mechanism of the graded school. How often we hear an anxious mother say: "The children are not taught spelling until the third grade, and the teacher tells me not to have my boy spell at home, as it interferes with the new reading method." Is not this the place for the mother to ask herself this question: is it possible that being a good speller is a hindrance to progress in school? If so, which is more important, the accommodation of the individual to a rigid school system or the ability to become an independent thinker?

Educators advance various reasons for the difficulties encountered in teaching children to spell. These discussions are called forth by the difficulties met in the grammar and high school in teaching this subject. Little trouble would arise if spelling were rigorously and properly taught in the primary school. We may say of the twelve-year-old or of the high-school pupil, "He does not spell because he is eye-minded, and must see the word before him in order to grasp it," or "He is ear-minded, and gets spelling from hearing rather than from the printed page," or "He is motor minded, and does not get a word from seeing or hearing it, but must repeat it frequently before it becomes fixed." These things are undoubtedly true at the high-school age, but there is no normal child who could not learn spelling if properly taught at the period between six to ten years.

Proper teaching includes due attention to pronunciation, enunciation, syllabication, training the ear to the letter sounds and to sound values. The best way is the simple, direct, commonsense way, delightfully old-fashioned in method and result.

While there is no desire to give a set plan for the mother to pursue, the following outline may prove an aid in the beginning. Does the mother distrust the simplicity of these homespun methods? They are being used with unexampled success by the most progressive teachers in America today. When the child has learned the alphabet devise games with the letters to teach him to spell. Sets of capital letters, each letter on a small cardboard square, may be made at home by the mother and child cutting out the letters from magazines and pasting them on cardboard. The arrangement of letters to form the child's name is a good beginning. Let him hunt out more letters and form the same word. This trains the eye and develops perseverance; it drills on the alphabet, and bridges the way from total ignorance of the structure of words to a knowledge of their formation. Building the names of members of the family, of playmates and playthings, seldom grows wearisome until the game has served its purpose.

But games dealing with words do not explain how to teach spelling itself. For a long time we ought to confine ourselves to the use of words of three letters. Testing different lists of words shows that the lists here given are the most satisfactory for the first lessons. Take in alphabetical order the words of three letters ending in "at": *bat, cat, fat, hat, mat, pat, rat, sat, tat, vat*. The entire list is given in this case as an example of the way the succeeding lists are to be made out. The child is taught orally to spell *cat* and is directed to find the letters and arrange them to form the word. Then he is taught one after another the succeeding words in this list, also spelling them out with the letters. From the first, distinctness of enunciation should be insisted upon, the word c-a-t being sounded so that each letter gets its full value. At this time the child's vocal organs are easily trained, and correct habits offset the likelihood of wretched oral habits later.

Several days or even weeks may be required in learning the above list, but please remember that if mastered now they are acquired for all time, and, what is also important, the habit of learning, which will make easier and easier the succeeding lessons, is being established.

We are then ready for the next list of words ending in "an": *an, ban, can, fan, man, pan, ran, tan, van*. The whole list should be taught as thoroughly and carefully as that preceding. They will probably be learned in half the time, since the only new sound is the final "n." Have the letter "n" distinctly sounded by the child so that he will observe the difference in its formation and sound from that of *m*.

While it might seem logical at this point to choose the series ending in *ad*, or *am*, the similarity of the *d* and *m* to the *n* sound seems to make it desirable to give the young child a series, instead, with a change in the vowel sound, and so we resort to the words rhyming with *it*.

it	bit	fit	
hit	pit	sit	wit

Easy as this transition may seem, there are difficulties sufficient to preclude the idea of disposing of the list at a sitting. The new vowel, the *w*, and the *h* sounds will need attention and practice for some time. The next series of *in* will be none the less difficult.

in	bin	din
fin	gin	pin
sin	tin	win

For a long time the child should spell each day all the words he has thus far been given, until they have become a vital part of his mental equipment. In no piece of work is it more unquestionably true that it is useless to go on to the new until the old has been learned thoroughly. In addition to these word lists for oral spelling the box of letters will be found invaluable. Show the child how to arrange a chosen list of words, then mix the letters and let him rearrange them. This is not requiring too much, if only the letters he needs for that list are placed before him. Many other schemes will unfold themselves to the earnest mother. But do not lose patience if the child does not seem to make rapid progress. In the beginning, of all times, we should proceed very slowly. If the child of five learns a single new word a day for the first year he is doing well. If in a five-year course a child learns one word a day the first year, two a day the second, three the third, four the fourth, and five the fifth, this amounts to his being able to spell four thousand five hundred words at the end of the period. This means a greater number of words than is comprised in an every-day vocabulary. If a child of five learns to spell a single new word each day, and goes ahead at the rate just indicated, at ten years of age he spells easily. He has a good vocabulary, a respect for correct spelling, and an eye and ear trained to sound and to the association of ideas. The child who is not a good speller for his age at ten is not likely to be a good speller for his age at twenty.

For a considerable time the child's spelling may be wisely confined to short words that have no silent letters. We may deviate but little from the plan of using word lists until the beginner is ready to spell the words from his reading. These lists gradually increase in difficulty. While the memory is plastic we should constantly direct the attention to the spelling of words. It is the greatest saving in time and energy to spell from those lists where only the letter or letters preceding the vowel are changed. Notice the slightly increasing difficulties in these words: *and, sand, stand, strand.* Until the child has had considerable training do not expect him to express initiative in spelling. We shall look for this in a reasonable time. Here is an exercise you can use with the greatest success: give the child the word *sing* and ask him to give the words that rhyme with it. He will think of *ring*, probably of *spring* and *string*. You will notice there are no new sounds in these words. Have him pronounce them clearly, and he usually spells them without further assistance. Here is where he is learning to reach ahead and do for himself instead of having the teacher lead him.

The following words fit in well with the work of a six-year-old. Always arrange the lists in alphabetical sequence. This makes for orderly classification that will be a great and unconscious help when the pupil comes to use the dictionary:

bad	bag	bay	cap	caw	bug	
cad	fag	day	gap	daw	dug	
dad	gag	fay	hap	jaw	hug	
fad	hag	gay	lap	law	jug	
gad	jag	hay	map	maw	lug	
had	lag	jay	nap	paw	mug	
lad	nag	lay	rap	raw	pug	
mad	rag	may	sap	saw	rug	
pad	sag	nay	tap		tug	
sad	tag	pay				
	wag	ray				
		say				
		way				
dip	big	bid	fly	cry	bow	cot

hip	dig	did	my	dry	cow	dot
lip	fig	hid	ply	fry	how	got
nip	gig	kid	shy	pry	mow	hot
rip	pig	lid	sky	try	now	jot
sip	rig	rid	sly		row	lot
tip	wig		spy		sow	not
			sty		vow	sot
			thy			tot
			why			

bun	bob	cog	fop	cod	bet
dun	cob	cog	hop	god	get
fun	fob	dog	lop	hod	jet
gun	hob	fog	mop	nod	let
pun	job	hog	sop	pod	met
run	mob	jog	top	rod	net

den	dew	bar	am	cub	up	ax
fen	few	car	dam	hub	cup	lax
hen	hew	far	ham	rub	pup	tax
men	mew	mar	jam	tub	sup	wax
pen	new	par	ram			
ten	pew	tar	yam			
wen						

bed	beg	boy	gum	but	bud	ox
fed	keg	coy	hum	cut	cud	box
led	leg	joy	rum	hut	mud	fox
red	peg	toy	sum	nut		

fix	dim
mix	him
six	rim

The above work is sufficient not only for weeks, but even for months. After the child has learned these words he easily masters longer ones. It is best, however, to keep up the practice of giving words that have no silent letters. The following lists, each consisting of from five to fifteen words, are given only in part. We should strive to have the child proceed independently in making these lists, after he has been given the key-word, as "and" in the first list. His words ought to be given him orally before they are written or formed with the paste-board letters, in order to avoid having a wrong word impressed upon his mind.

and	end	bent	art	belt	camp	bind
band	bend	cent	cart	felt	damp	find
hand	fend	dent	dart	melt	lamp	hind
land	lend	lent	mart	pelt	cramp	kind
sand	mend	pent	part	welt	clamp	mind
strand	rend	sent	chart	smelt		
bland	send	tent	start			
brand	tend	vent	smart			
grand	vend	went				
gland	wend	scent				
	blend	spent				
	spend					

ant	bound	out	old
pant	found	gout	bold
rant	hound	lout	cold
scant	mound	pout	fold
grant	pound	shout	gold

By this time the child may learn words containing occasional silent letters:

ate	bane	fade	age	ale	came
date	cane	made	cage	bale	dame

fate lane wade page dale fame
gate mane blade rage gale game

ape cave bare less bore
cape gave care mess core
tape lave dare bless fore
shape nave fare chess gore

all ell ill gilt beck cull
ball bell bill hilt deck dull
call cell fill silt neck gull
fall dell gill tilt peck hull

bull bolt cord count hole dome
full colt ford fount mole home
pull dolt lord mount pole tome

cope dove carp bard bake oil
hope love harp card cake boil
lope glove sharp hard lake coil
mope shove lard make foil

dine bide eat hung cool beet
fine hide beat lung fool feet
kine ride feat rung pool meet

bee beam urn ear fight ink
fee ream burn dear light king
lee seam turn fear might link

dish camp kept ire bank deep
fish damp wept dire dank peep
wish lamp slept fire lank weep

arm best bump our ace
farm lest dump hour dace
harm nest hump sour lace

While the child is acquiring the above lists he may also learn to add "s," "ing," and "ed" to a word, such as *land—lands, landing, landed*. According to the plan given for teaching reading, the child has memorized by this time parts of the poem "Hiawatha." He may now have spelling-lessons taken from this poem, learning each day a few words that have no especial difficulty. You may allow the child to make its own lists, taking the words from "Hiawatha," or from the story of Rip Van Winkle, or from any good literature. The child will seldom be dishonest about the words it chooses by selecting easy or familiar ones. On the other hand, it will not write a foolishly long list. An assignment of this kind is a test of judgment as well as an exercise in spelling. The child of eight or nine should spell at all convenient times. His mother may hear his lessons and give him an occasional new word at odd moments while she works about the house. A very busy mother can hear the child's lessons while she is darning or ironing. She can teach him to spell the names of familiar objects about the house and yard. The mother who examines these lists will not consider them a formidable assignment for the child to master by the age of nine or ten, yet the child who enters school for the first time at this age equipped with the knowledge and training indicated by this brief outline, if given a fair chance, will hold his own among children who entered the school at six.

VIII

HOW TO TEACH ARITHMETIC

No doubt arithmetic has had its full share of prominence among the obligatory subjects in every school curriculum. Not only has more attention been given to it, but frequently twice as much time as is allotted to the teaching of other subjects, and in addition a too generous apportionment of home preparation. The results are admittedly poor, and call for adjustment and betterment. There is no quarrel with those who place arithmetic among the essentials of elementary teaching. The objection is to the prevailing method and system.

Arithmetic will not demand much time nor worry for the six-year-old. He is getting a sense of number without direct teaching. He is learning to count, perhaps to ten, perhaps to one hundred, but just so far as his ambition carries him. He may count people, toys, animals, birds, pennies. He may make change for a nickel, possibly for a dime. Knowing the cost of a two-cent stamp, he may study out the cost of two or three stamps, but his mind should not be puzzled and confused with numbers. That work is most unimportant now, especially if he does not evince an eagerness for it.

The number sense, one of the latest to appear, comes only through natural development. The process cannot be hastened; and even if it could, there would be no particular gain in so doing. To the little child twenty means no more than three, while one hundred is just a name. A small girl will tell you there were more than a million people on the street-corner as she came by, and that she is kept awake nights by a thousand cats in the back yard. Since numbers are so meaningless, do not imagine you can teach arithmetic to the child or hasten very much his understanding of the subject. He must learn by actually counting different objects many times. If you attempt to teach a small child all the arithmetic assigned by the course of study to his years, you will so hopelessly confuse him that you defeat your own purpose. The child at six is entering the mental stage corresponding to the beginnings of civilization. Like primitive man, he has little use for or comprehension of numbers beyond five or ten, perhaps twenty, and does not grasp the meaning of higher numbers. By way of rote you could at this time, or earlier, teach him combinations of higher numbers to a considerable extent; yet the problematical benefit is not worth the labor. It has been demonstrated that we have to work for a year to teach a six-year-old child what he could learn by his own efforts in a single month when he is eight years of age. The child at ten is just as far in advance and fully as good a student of arithmetic if he commences his study at eight rather than at six.

The age at which a child may best begin the study of arithmetic depends chiefly upon its individual mental development, and will manifest itself by a very apparent interest in counting. When your boy asks, "What comes after eleven?" or "What comes after nineteen?" you may safely begin to teach him. No text-book is needed. Number work is to be direct, simple, logical, and fitted to the child's needs. It is not to be taught as a matter of memory, but is to be worked out step by step by the learner.

It is not too much to say that in no other subject do teachers commit so many pedagogical crimes, or go so directly counter to the laws of child-psychology and of mind growth, as in the teaching of arithmetic. One of the hardest things for the teacher is to let the child alone, let him make mistakes and unmake them, trust his intelligence, his growing sense. She should direct, not merely control. She should advise, not merely dictate. We sacrifice one of the main points, the use of judgment, the practice of thinking, in order to save time. It is here that a talkative teacher should be muzzled and an officiously helpful one handcuffed. The work of the teacher in the beginning is to show the child how to work, to help himself, to give him in this way a fair start. Then the teacher should assume an alert passivity, merely watchful, very rarely directly helping, but occasionally directing discreetly. The child will then develop independence and initiative that shall gain in momentum as he grows into manhood. The highest and noblest purpose of the teacher has been obtained when the child has been taught to be an independent, resourceful thinker and worker.

How, then, are we to teach arithmetic? The child, as we have said, already counts to twenty or thereabouts, and is interested in the process. The first step is to teach counting by twos. Let him find suitable objects of any kind—buttons, or pennies, or pebbles. There are several reasons for choosing the latter. They do not cost money. They are natural objects, and any child can get them. Then for the sake of learning what numbers actually are, the learner will count with the pebbles until he no longer needs them, at which time he will abandon them as readily as a snake sheds its skin.

Show him how to arrange the pebbles in twos, and how to count them as such—thus, 2, 4, 6. This will be as far as the first lessons go, because the arranging and counting has to be done several times. The counting downward by removing pebbles—6, 4, 2—follows. In these lessons a new idea has entered into the child's mind. Give it ample time to germinate. Five or ten minutes is sufficient time for each of the first lessons. The great idea for pupil and teacher is the fact that to-morrow must find the pupil farther advanced than today. If today he counted to six, tomorrow he shall count to six and to eight. The next day the lesson starts in this way again, and the pupil is permitted to build farther than eight; he proceeds to ten. Although this may seem a trifling advance, the lesson learned in itself is not inconsiderable—it is the most important to be drawn from this subject at this time—that we are building, and that tomorrow must find us farther advanced than today. The counting downward from eight, etc., continues, and involves no small mental effort. Account of the number of twos used should be taken, preferably of the pupil's own accord. But the memory need not be forced to retain the fact that four twos are eight. So the work continues, a short lesson each day, each marking unquestionable advancement. At the end of a few weeks, spending five or ten minutes a day in this manner, the child will readily count upward and downward by the twos as far as twenty, thirty, or forty—just so far as he goes readily and joyfully.

So much for the first steps, simple indeed, but a distinct part of the fundamental structure. Next we would teach or rather show the child how to learn the multiplication table of twos. For this our pebbles are the only requisite material. Begin with the two twos. Tell the child to place two twos on the table, and he will understand you. Do not bother about one two. This is obvious to the child. He places the two twos and tells you there are four. Then arranging three twos, he gives the result as six. As in the counting, we shall not go very far the first day, since our main object is not the acquisition of certain numerical facts, but the learning how to work, how to do for one's self. When tomorrow comes we will start again with the two-table from the beginning, with each tomorrow getting a little farther. In a few weeks the child will know this table as far as 12×2, upward and downward.

While the distinction may seem trifling, there is, as a matter of fact, a vast difference between learning the table of twos, as 2×4, 2×5, etc., or this, the better way, 4×2, 5×2, etc. For this is the foundation whereon the child will build all the succeeding tables, which he is to work out by the process of addition. The second manner indicated shows him clearly that multiplication is nothing but a peculiar kind of addition. Just as the four fundamental processes of arithmetic—addition, subtraction, multiplication, and division—are more important than anything that follows in mathematics, so these first lessons as here outlined merit careful consideration. Do not hurry the child. What is there to hurry toward? Here, even more than in other studies, the individual is to strike his own gait. If the work prescribed above is accomplished in two weeks, very good. If, on the other hand, it moves slowly and six weeks are consumed in the task, good again. Great minds are usually of slow growth, just as the giant oak reaches maturity gradually. If the child evinces an interest in this work and goes on with it ever so ploddingly, you may be content.

We arrive now at another stage, which differs from the preceding in two respects—the work is of increasing difficulty; the teacher's part becomes more and more apparently passive. The child learns to count by threes, using the objects as before, proceeding slowly as in the first instance, mastering thoroughly the work of each day, going a little farther each day, getting just a little more self-active and a little less dependent upon the instructor. For the first lesson in the threes, twelve is quite far enough; the table is learned both upward and downward, this constituting a good practical lesson in addition and subtraction. He may look about for objects presenting groups of threes—clover leaves, the trillium, the prongs of a fork, etc. Quite likely in another week he will count by threes up to thirty or even farther, and downward. At this point it would not be amiss to direct the learner's attention to the important fact that, although this task is a larger one than the study of the twos, he has mastered it in a shorter time because of having: done the first one well. You cannot begin too early to impress him with the great lesson that every day and every duty are the steppingstones to greater days and greater duties.

Of course you know that an up-to-date teacher would advise you at this stage to use concrete problems at every step. Four cows and three cows are how many cows? At two cents each, what will seven apples cost? The specific objection to the concrete problem as a main issue is that it makes so much talk when the child might better be thinking and working out these things for himself. The problems of the pebbles before him are as good as cow problems for present purposes. He is getting acquainted with numbers. However, it would be well to find time to "play store" with him.

Next comes the multiplication table of threes, produced and

learned with objects, step by step, as before, until mastered to 12×3, and occupying perhaps a week.

This closes one distinct phase of the individual plan, and marks the place where the teacher steps down and away, in so far as actually setting the child his lesson. Thus far she has labored with him, but always with an eye to the moment when he is to move ahead with a certain assumption of responsibility. The time is coming, and but a few months distant, when this child may be left to himself for half an hour quite without books or a set lesson, and required to produce a fitting piece of work. The accomplishment of this result is simply a matter of patient training, and the chief requisite for the teacher is the self control to refrain from doing for the child work that he should do for himself.

The twos and threes being learned, addition, subtraction, and multiplication tables, you may well say to the child, "What shall we do next?" As we are dealing with a child above six years of age, we will expect him to suggest the fours. Then set him the task of counting by fours, possibly to sixteen for the first lesson. He is to have no assistance, but must be allowed his own time. The time element is not to enter into these lessons for the present, since speed must be secondary to accuracy, and subordinate to the formation of habit. The pupil is cultivating the work habit, and we should introduce no more than one problem at a time. In the course of two or three more lessons the child may count to forty by four's. Even in reciting these lessons the demand for speed should not be made, except as it is naturally justified after many repetitions of the work. Far better is the recurring mental effort required to call up each succeeding number—as it was discovered originally with the aid of the pebbles. After another year or two, or with beginners nine or ten years of age, special drills for rapidity may be given, of which we shall speak in another chapter.

Let us suppose, then, that at the end of three months the child knows how to count by twos, threes, and fours, to fifty or thereabouts and down, and that he knows the respective multiplication tables to 12×4. He may now learn the fives in like manner, especially if he starts to do so without suggestion. But because of larger numbers being involved in the tables, it seems better to start, at this period, along another line dealing with numbers within his horizon. From now on the pupil should have a note-book, in which he writes the lesson learned each day, with the date. This may represent the final lesson just mentioned:

January 26, 1914.

4	
8	2×4 = 8
12	3×4 = 12
16	4×4 = 16
	etc.

When this has been accomplished we ought to begin a series of lessons which will prove most attractive to the child, and whose purpose will be explained more fully later on. The teacher is again in evidence until the new line of work is well under way. We begin by taking six pebbles and requiring the child to divide them into groups of twos, so as to ascertain how many twos there are in six. He may then be taught to write the statement in his note-book, thus: 6÷2=3. Explain the meaning of the symbols in this statement, and teach him to read it. After this point is clear, tell him next to divide the pebbles into groups of threes, and have this written 6÷3=2, under the previous statement. The next step is to ascertain how many fours there are in six. The result may be written:

6 ÷ 4 = 1 and 2 remain (the number remaining being called the remainder)
6 ÷ 5 = 1 and 1 remains
6 ÷ 6 = 1

But no statement is written down here or later until the result has been ascertained by actual count. This is an example of the day's work in arithmetic for a period covering many weeks. Today the number is six; tomorrow we shall take seven; the next day eight. Some of the advantages of work thus planned are the following:

Every day marks a distinct step, and one of increasing difficulty. Yet the difficulty is not sufficient to justify the pupil in looking for help or the teacher in proffering it.

The analysis of each number in this way, in conjunction with a plan to be given later, makes the child so familiar with these numbers that each is clearly and distinctly visualized.

This series helps to realize the educator's ideal of efficient schooling—a minimum of direction on the part of the teacher producing the maximum of response from the pupil.

The teacher's part must be, indeed, a passive one. Rarely will she need to make a suggestion, give a direction, or require a correction. Here and there a word such as, "Well done," "This looks better than yesterday's, the columns are straighter, the figures neater," will be in place. A mistake must not be tolerated. It is assumed that the work is not given to a child that is incapable of the effort demanded, so that a mistake must be considered as arising from carelessness. Strict measures in the beginning are a true kindness. When a mistake is made do not permit an erasure; blue-pencil the entire lesson and require all of it to be worked again.

After two or three weeks the child may be shown a concise way of stating the remainder in division, thus:

$$16 \div 3 = 5^{1/3}$$
$$16 \div 4 = 4$$
$$16 \div 5 = 3^{1/5}$$

It would not be wise at this time to endeavor to teach him anything further concerning the fractional form, as we are to avoid any explanations or details that might result in confusion to the pupil's mind. This is only a step toward the understanding of fractions that will be helpful a few months later. Still another step is to teach the child that division is expressed by the form 20/2, so that he will work out the analysis of 20, arranging it in this form:

$$20 \div 2 = \frac{20}{2} = 10$$

$$20 \div 3 = \frac{20}{3} = 6^{2/3}$$

$$20 \div 4 = \frac{20}{4} = 5$$

$$20 \div 5 = \frac{20}{5} = 4$$

$$20 \div 6 = \frac{20}{6} = 3^{2/6}$$

And this form as well:

$$22 \div 2 = \tfrac{1}{2} \text{ of } 22 = \frac{22}{6} = 11$$

$$22 \div 3 = \tfrac{1}{3} \text{ of } 22 = \frac{20}{6} = 7^{1/3}$$

It is evident that these two lessons will help clear up the difficulties usually encountered in the teaching of fractions.

The immense advantage of such a continuously developed plan of number work is at once apparent. In it is comprised recurring practice and drill in the four elementary operations; each day's work is somewhat more difficult and more comprehensive than the preceding. The lessons increase in length so gradually that the child, with his increasing capacity, finds himself able to complete the lesson assigned each day. The work is logical and clear to the child's mind, tempting him at every step to try his powers by doing more than is demanded. It is possible to place upon the child a measure of responsibility to the extent that a teacher's absence does not justify the child in being idle for lack of knowing what is expected of him. There could be no better method of cultivating the habit of work and of concentration in the child than by teaching him in this way to master arithmetic.

The practice of dividing each successive number by each smaller number as far as a divisor which is approximately half the number divided, as:

$$40 \div 2 =$$
$$40 \div 3 =$$
$$\text{to}$$
$$40 \div 20 =$$

may be continued until the child has become very accurate and no longer resorts to objects to prove the answers. The use of objects is usually abandoned by the child somewhere between the numbers 25 and 50. Then instead of measuring every successive number one may use alternate numbers. Or if the child has shown accuracy and speed in measuring 66 as far as $66 \div 33$, let him take 70 for the next dividend—and now the assigned lesson may be, since the divisors are numerous, "Work to the bottom of the page"—of the notebook.

How far this work is to be continued depends upon the child, some working only to 150, some to 300. At any rate, it has involved such practice in mental arithmetic that a solid, sure foundation is being laid for future instruction and progress. There can be no better mental training than to sit down and think out a new table, whether it be the fours or the twenty-fours.

Here is another helpful scheme that may be used when the pupil shows a readiness to profit thereby. Take cards of bristol-board, 3 inches by 5 inches—or clean pasteboard will do—and write on them in large, distinct figures the following forty-five combinations. Use both sides, one combination on each.

9 9 9 9 9 9 9 9 9 8 8 8 8 8 8 8 8 7 7 7 7 7 7 7
9 8 7 6 5 4 3 2 1 8 7 6 5 4 3 2 1 7 6 5 4 3 2 1

6 6 6 6 6 6 5 5 5 5 5 4 4 4 4 3 3 3 2 2 1
6 5 4 3 2 1 5 4 3 2 1 4 3 2 1 3 2 1 2 1 1

These cards may first be used as drill in addition, and their regular employment five minutes a day so trains the child that he instantly comes to recognize 7+8 =15. Again let me emphasize: accuracy comes first in importance. First give the child plenty of time to ascertain the right answer. The next day it will not take so long.

Next these cards are used for practice on the multiplication table, and if you have two or three children learning them at once, so much the better. Lead them to see something more than the mere product of numbers shown; they will recognize not only that four 5's are 20, but also that it is the same as two 10's, and the same as three 6's and 2 more. This is what we are after—independent thinking and initiative. Show the child your approval of his using his brains in finding a new way to solve a problem. For example, ask a boy how he will find 24×25. He tells you: "I shall get ten 25's and ten 25's and four 25's." Another boy says: "Get four 25's and then six times that." You may possibly give them a short method of finding the result, but present it to them as something to compare with their previous knowledge and judge as to its advantages, not as something to be unthinkingly adopted for all time. This plan of the number cards may be carried farther advantageously to 2 the card with 25
25

To retrace our steps. After the child has gone as far in this work of division as twenty or there-abouts he is to resume the study of the multiplication table, and continue it, paralleling the division of the different numbers. Thus the tables are so much used and reviewed that with the completion of memorizing them to 12×12 and farther they have become fixed in the mind. Nor should we stop with 12×5 or 12×9. The child ought to be taught to employ the tables very much farther. For example, if he has difficulty in dividing 75 by 4, suggest that he get it from the multiplication table, and that he begin perhaps with 12×4 and go forward until he ascertains how many fours in 75.

The child has already learned either incidentally or from your teaching the meaning of ½. This fraction is used more frequently in life than any other, and we shall use it in many ways. After some oral practice in finding halves, tell him to write in his book ½ of numbers to 25, thus:

$$\frac{1}{2} \text{ of } 2 = 1$$
$$\frac{1}{2} \text{ of } 3 = 1^{1/2}, \text{ etc.}$$

Next let him write multiplication tables of $2^{1/2}$, as:

$$2 \times 2^{1/2} = 5$$
$$3 \times 2^{1/2} = 7^{1/2}, \text{ etc.}$$

of $3^{1/2}$, or $4^{1/2}$, and so on, until the work is entirely clear to him.

Before going any farther with pure number work give the child a clear idea of measure, unit, and measuring. Take anything for a unit: a piece of stick, a pencil, the span of a hand, etc. Let the child measure the length of a table in pencil lengths by finding out how many times it contains the length of the pencil. Let us assume the child finds $8^{1/2}$ times. Then the length of the table is $8^{1/2}$ pencil lengths, meaning, of course, some definite pencil. Having repeated this process with various objects, show the child the inconvenience of having different units, and that on account of this inconvenience we have agreed on standard units of length, as the foot, yard, inch, etc. This same process is successively applied to other kinds of measure: money, weight, etc.

Here the foot-rule may be used to good advantage, as the basis of a table:

feet		inches
1	=	12
½	=	
$1^{1/2}$	=	
2	=	
$2^{1/2}$	=	etc.

Thus far would I explain and write it, and then tell the child to continue it by himself, perhaps the length of the page. He sees a natural reason for a stopping-place at the bottom of the page, but only an artificial one if we invariably say, go as far as 12, or 20, or 30, etc.

A line of work that seems as potent in arousing the curiosity and interest of most children as it is helpful is finding the factors of numbers, from the beginning to 100 or 200, or until the lesson seems to have served its purpose. A child of eight will understand clearly enough what is meant by *factors* when you explain that $3\times7=21$, and that 3 and 7 are said to be the factors of 21; that $9\times8=72$, and that 9 and 8 are factors of 72.

Start the pupil on this work by making him write the numbers in columns, with the factors opposite, as:

$$4 = 2\times2$$
$$6 = 2\times3, \text{etc.}$$

A little discussion will bring out the idea that such numbers as 2, 3, or 5, that have no factors but themselves and one, must not be in the list; yet, instead of simply omitting these, we place them at the bottom of the page, in what we term the scrap-basket, giving them their right name, "prime numbers." Here are two new terms, "factors" and "prime numbers"; no confusion need result from giving to the factored numbers their proper name, "composite numbers," and writing it at the top of each page.

The child who, taking all pains possible, has done the number work thus outlined will rarely make, in this kind of lesson, a mistake other than discarding somewhat freely the composite numbers he has failed to recognize as such. The teacher should not rectify the error when she discovers it, but set him hunting among his list of prime numbers for numbers that have factors.

While the purpose of this work is very far indeed from making play out of number work, these lessons contain the elements that make fascinating—because within its power—to the inquiring mind a game, a puzzle, an undertaking that promises to be just beyond its reach if pupil and teacher have not been alert, zealous, and persistent. At every step it calls forth effort.

No terms are defined other than those based on preceding work. The definitions of factor, prime number, composite number, etc., must not be given to the child until he has had considerable experience in working with them so that they are then given as names of known objects, as of a street or an individual.

After a week or two spent on this work we may proceed a little further in considering other easy fractions. By cutting up an apple, teach the halves and fourths and their relations to each other. With the pebbles require the child to take 8, and find 1/2, 1/4, 2/4, 3/4, 4/4. You are not to draw his deductions for him, nor very much hasten the process by which he concludes that 1/2 of a number equals 2/4, nor that 4/4 equals the whole number. The next day he may take 12, and find these same fractional parts, and so with successive numbers until he has learned by degrees all you would have him learn about these fractions and without interference. While this step with the fractions may seem unnecessary in view of the practice given in measuring numbers, as

$$14 \div 2 = \tfrac{1}{2} \text{ of } 14 = 7$$

the child sees the fraction in a different setting and a different light, and must make his own discoveries. In his note-book will be found such a page, worked, of course, by himself:

1/2 of 24 = 12
1/4 of 24 = 6
2/4 of 24 = 12
3/4, etc.
4/4, etc.

1/2 of 36 = 18
1/4 of 36 =
2/4 of 36
3/4, etc.
4/4, etc.

A reason for employing the entire group of fourths for an extended period in this number work is the immense advantage gained, and later on manifesting itself when the child in the midst of examples in fractions, meeting a problem involving ¾, automatically associates it with ¼; a process simple in itself, yet an ever-present stumbling-block even in our grammar and high schools.

There need be no difficulty now in going to ⅛. For this a sheet of paper may be folded into halves and fourths, and further into eighths. Do not hurry over this. The child learns by doing and by observing that in the whole sheet of paper there are 8/8; 1/2 of it 4/8, 2/8. Let him work this out.

As a method to bring about familiarity with fractional relations the following is proposed. Start the child thus:

$$\tfrac{1}{2} = \frac{\quad}{4} = \frac{\quad}{8} = \frac{\quad}{16} = \text{etc.}$$

and so on across the page, he writing the equivalents. Next, tell him to work ¼ in this way:

$$\tfrac{1}{4} = \frac{\quad}{8} = \frac{\quad}{16} = \text{etc.}$$

Then continue with 2/4, 3/4, and 4/4, unless the child understands so readily the purport that only 3/4 need be considered.

Now let him work with 1/8 and all the eighths in the same manner. If the fourths have been reduced to 32^{nds}, the 8^{ths} may be reduced to 64^{ths}, or to a still smaller unit. Any difficulty in the comprehension of the work, given here or farther on, can only arise from the fact that the pupil's mind is not yet ready for it.

Tables may be constructed from time to time that give practical drill in fractions, using again and again the foot-rule:

feet		inches
1/2	=	
1/4	=	
2/4	=	
feet		inches
3/4	=	

4/4	=	
$1^{1/4}$	=	
$1^{3/4}$	=	
$2^{1/4}$	=	etc.

the child carrying this table further by additional numbers in the first column.

Use also tables like this:

yards		inches
1	=	
1/2	=	
1/4	=	
$1^{1/4}$	=	
$1^{3/4}$	=	
$2^{1/2}$	=	etc.

At this time the child is getting considerable practice in actual measuring. With a foot-rule he finds the dimensions of tables, rugs, the porch, and yard. Problems such as the following may be assigned: find the length in inches or feet of the four sides of the tables; in feet, of a room; the house; the length of a rope reaching around the room; around the four sides of the yard or the house.

Now has come the time to teach 1/3 by cutting a pie, by folding papers, by separating pebbles into three *equal* parts, always emphasizing the word "equal."

yards		inches
1/3	=	
2/3	=	
3/3	=	
$1^{1/3}$	=	etc.

Reverting again to the constant practice in counting, the child may learn to count by twos, beginning with 1, thus 1-3-5, to 100, and downward; next by threes, beginning with 1, as 1-4-7 to about

100 and backward. Then begin with 2, as 2-5-8, etc., to 100 or thereabouts. Some of this practice may be used every day, along with the concrete problems described; it is not essential that this counting be written down, but if so, let it be kept in the book and dated.

Thus the practice goes on:

by 4's –	1	2	3
	5	6	7
	9	10	11, etc.
by 5's –	1	2	3
	6	7	8
	11	12	13
	16	17	18

For weeks this kind of drill may be kept in sight, taking a fresh start each day. Being systematic, it gives the child opportunity to plan and think ahead for himself. He will know now that the sixes are to be learned, and that if he begins with one to-day he will begin with two to-morrow.

The following is a good table in concrete work that may be used at this point:

pounds		ounces
1	=	16
1/2	=	
1/4	=	
1/8	=	
$2^{1/2}$	=	
3	=	
4	=	
5	=	
1/16	=	

This is another good table that he may have.

rods		feet
1	=	$16^{1/2}$
2	=	
3	=	
4	=	
5	=	
6	=	
1/2	=	
1/4	=	
1/8	=	

This may be carried farther by combining the whole number and the fraction, as in the other tables, as far as the teacher sees fit to go.

The work so far may have taken from one to two years, depending upon the child. He might well start in here to learn the meaning of a square—a square inch, a square foot. He will get these by actually marking out the spaces on paper and cutting out square inches and square feet. This is even better than his having ready made squares and simply putting them together. He can cut several square inches and arrange them into squares and oblongs. When once he has learned by making it that a square inch is represented by an area one inch long and one inch wide he can place two such squares side by side and measure two square inches. He can cut out several of these inch squares so as to form oblongs of the required number of inches, such as 1×3, 2×3, 3×3. In the latter he may notice that he has a square containing nine square inches. Then he may start with an oblong, 1"×4", 2"×4", 3"×4", until he has a 4-inch square and 16 square inches. He will not reach this point in one day, nor in two days. He will be set marking much good paper into squares and cutting these squares very accurately. Failing to do this, he will be directed to cut more. There is a purpose in this paper-cutting, too, for he is going to use the squares. He may get a sufficiently large number to make 5 and 6 inch squares. He may find how many of these inch squares are necessary to cover one side of a book, a table, etc. Now with his ruler he may carefully construct a square, one foot on each side, and later cut out a sufficient number of inch squares to fill this space. In this way he discovers for himself that there are 144 square inches in a square foot. An acquaintance with the square foot brings the child good material for a series of valuable lessons. He knows by actual work and count that one square foot contains 144 square inches. After the practice he has had in constructing other tables it will be interesting to see to what extent he can construct this table based on the square foot, bringing in very many of the fractional parts, the fourths, eighths, sixteenths, thirds, ninths, sixths, twelfths. He will also begin the task of drawing a square foot and dividing it accurately into square inches. This is quite an undertaking, and one would scarcely expect satisfactory results with the first attempt. Many attempts will quite likely be made before this square foot is divided into the 144 square inches with sufficient accuracy to justify its acceptance as a piece of work.

It is unnecessary to outline here all of the problems and all of the practices in number work, especially in simple fractions, that can be based on this one lesson. There is good material in this for three or four weeks' work in arithmetic, and the planning of that work will not be the least enjoyable and profitable employment for teacher and pupil. The teacher should give directions only where they are needed. She may suggest a line of work which the child can profitably continue by himself for at least one day. For instance, "What can you find out about one-third of that square foot?"

This work will be the basis for surface measurement. With the foot square of paper as a unit, the pupil may measure table-tops, rugs, floors, either by repeating the one unit or cutting out many so as to cover the surface.

Do not think that because the child has learned to measure lines he is ready for the measurement of surfaces, nor that cubic measure immediately follows on the heels of linear and square measure. The little child who can measure lines and surfaces is no more ready for the measurement of solids than he is for the theory of limits. Let him alone until he grows up to this many-sided affair. And when his mind has reached that state of preparedness through physical and mental contact and the desire for understanding there is nothing, absolutely nothing, to the teaching of solid measure. In a day he grasps it. Your neighbor may tell you that her little girl is only nine, and has learned "denominate numbers" in school. How has she learned them? Why, the teacher hammers in such facts as these: If you want to find AREA you multiply length by breadth; if you want to find cubical contents you multiply length, breadth, and thickness together. And that is as much as it means to the youngster.

Do not worry about long division. It is an abstract formula that has no active value in mind-training. It is one of the things the schools are always hoping to "rationalize"—to make concrete, so that the immature mind may grasp the very reason you "subtract, bring down the next figure, and divide again." They will never succeed. It remains an abstract formula even to the grown-ups, who find it a matter of habituation rather than of rationalization. Rarely should a child be taught long division before the tenth year. Why work hard to teach him at eight what he will learn easily in half the time at ten?

One of the most prevalent pedagogical crimes in the teaching of arithmetic consists in the practice of assigning work, conducting recitations, and planning courses without keeping in mind the eventual freeing of the child from the necessity of having the teacher plan his work. In a plain and simple way arithmetic may be made the ready and attractive means of leading to independence of thought and action. In the usual way of teaching it would be hopeless to ask of the child to consider and tell you what would be a reasonable assignment for the ensuing lesson, except as he might turn to the book and estimate the quantity of printed questions he could master, and then he would consider the space to be covered. A child of eight, on the other hand, sensibly trained in oral arithmetic can work by itself and may be profitably and reasonably required to prepare a daily lesson without dependence upon teacher, book, or specific instruction beyond a single suggestion. Even that need not be given more than once a week in order to provide adequate work and training for several lessons. The work of the teacher is chiefly to supervise and correct wrong tendencies of mental growth before they become fixed, just as you would watch the growing tree and help it to become straight. The great proportion of the arithmetic for these years at home will be mental, the kind that sharpened our grandfathers' wits, and the lack of which has hastened the downward tendency of modern schools.

IX

HOW TO TEACH WRITING AND DRAWING

ART is the outward manifestation, by means of skill and taste, of alert observation and a highly imaginative life. This implies the doing of things with ease and correctness, as it was understood by the great Italian painter Giotto, who was asked to send the Pope some proof of his art. The artist, who had given the world everlasting proofs of his art, first resented such a request. When pressed, he called for a piece of paper, took his pencil, and drew—a circle, with its center. The courtier refused to take this to his Holiness; the artist insisted. The Holy Father received the drawing, looked at it, smiled at the crestfallen courtier, and asked for a pair of compasses. "No artist ever produced, nor ever will produce, such a perfect work of art," said his Holiness, when, after applying the compasses, he found the circle to be absolutely correct. "Go to the artist and thank him for the lesson he has taught me." How many weary hours, days, months, and years must the great artist have spent to acquire such wonderful skill and easy grace.

The term art, as applied to the pursuits recognized under that name, like other figurative terms, is not extremely accurate. The thing which we usually understand by art is far from the plain, unmistakable thing defined in terms of Webster. By the word art is meant no more primarily than the power of performing certain actions acquired by experience, study, and observation. So when we speak of a work of art we really mean a product of the skill existing in the trained mind and trained muscles of the artist.

If then we think of art in terms of skill, of dexterity, of ingenuity, of the ability to adapt things in the natural world to our own uses, we are better prepared to seek the source of art in self-activity rather than in measured instruction. There is true art in an arithmetic lesson well done, in a reading-lesson well done, in planting a garden, hoeing the potatoes, in training a woodbine, in preparing a meal. Any lesson, any good piece of work, will serve to train mind and muscle to act in harmony. Therefore in this chapter on writing and drawing we shall consider even drawing as coming under the head of art only so far as the foregoing and kindred lessons and tasks merit being so classified. We shall consider drawing primarily as a further means of training the eye to see, the muscles to act.

Can art, or, rather, can the rudiments of art be taught to a child under ten years of age? They can, and can be taught so simply and thoroughly that the normally developed child will take to them as the duckling will take to water. And if art is considered in terms of skill, of dexterity, of ingenuity, it may well take its beginning in writing and drawing. Writing, as required of the child in the following lessons, represents a good piece of work every day, steady improvement in results, and gain in the power of co-ordination of hand and eye. Drawing, as the means of developing human ingenuity, contrivance, and self-expression, begins in a different way, and is carried on quite differently, yet side by side with the work in writing. They balance each other—the strict discipline of writing and the freedom of drawing. A child may be drawing from the time he is able to hold a pencil. Writing, since it is training in precision, should not begin before six or seven, or as soon thereafter as the mother is prepared to devote ten or fifteen minutes every day to the child's work. The time to begin does not relate in any way to what is being done in other lessons, such as reading or arithmetic, any more than to garden work or swimming.

In the teaching of writing and drawing we shall not discuss the forms of sense-training advocated by Montessori as leading to these branches, since these and allied activities belong to the kindergarten period. Anything and everything advocated by this great teacher pertaining to the tactile and motor senses is good. Writing, as an imitative art, necessarily involves rules, just as does any other occupation or business requiring skill, such as the art of building or engraving, the art of navigation, of baseball, of cooking, and we shall begin with the rules. They need not be considered formidable in any way. They are merely organized modes of operation serving to facilitate the performance of certain actions. We live in a world where we are necessarily hedged in by rules and laws. He who learns to conform to rules gains freedom in the end through self-control. Nor need they have a deadening effect on the child's spirit. The rule that says to forty children, "You are to remain inactive in those patent seats for three or six hours a day," is an unjust rule. But the rule that says, "You are to follow these instructions implicitly for ten or fifteen minutes," is not unjust; it is an exercise in self-control.

The writing-teacher must ever have in mind the object of teaching, which is not so much to impart knowledge as mental and physical discipline, the training to act in accordance with well-established fundamental rules, the accustoming to systematic and regular action, the desire to do, the habit of order and self-control. She will, therefore, insist on strict observance of the following rules, and will consider the mere form and shape of the letters of secondary importance.

(These instructions are addressed to the child through the teacher.)

I. Sit squarely before your desk or table on a seat very slightly sloping back, and just high enough to place the slightly raised elbow on the table.

II. Write with both elbows on the table, so that your body is evenly balanced and no curvature of the spine is possible.

III. Do not lean against the desk with the chest.

IV. Write from the very beginning with ink, so that you may learn to think and consider before you write. "What is written stands."

V. Do not erase bad writing; keep it before your eyes as a deterring example, and try to write better and take pleasure in your daily progress and improvement. (There is nothing more pernicious to the right mental development of a child than the promiscuous use of rubbers for erasing. Rubber-tipped pencils in the hand of a little child are just as abominable as chewing-gum in its little mouth. Both tend to cripple self-control. The old abominable slate-pencil effectively combined both.)

VI. Place your paper or book, well focused, exactly in front of you, slightly slanting to the left if you prefer slanting writing, perpendicularly to the edge of the desk if you prefer perpendicular writing. (Slanting and perpendicular here are a matter of taste. The author prefers slanting writing, basing this preference on results obtained.)

VII. Rest your right arm on its elbow, using the latter as a pivot, and support it by the tip of the fourth finger.

VIII. Hold your pen-holder between thumb and second finger, the first finger being used only to give pressure downward.

IX. Let your pen-holder point toward your right shoulder.

X. The pen-holder should be about six inches long, about 5/16 of an inch thick, and with a soft cover (cork or inflated rubber) at the lower end, slightly increasing in thickness to within about $1^{1/2}$ inches from the lower end, and then gradually tapering to the upper end.

XI. The tips of the fingers should be from $1^{1/2}$ inches to two inches from the point of the nib.

XII. The nib should be soft, and neither too blunt nor too sharp.

XIII. In writing both points of the nib should touch the paper, so the ink easily flows out of the nib without scratching or sputtering.

XIV. The left hand, with fingers not too close together, and nearer to the body than the right, should hold the paper or book firmly in place, changing its position to one farther from the body than the right hand when the writing approaches the lower edge of the paper.

7.
8.
9.
10.
(Start here)
11.
12.

13.

14.

15.

16.

17.

18.

19.

20.

21.

22.

23.

24.

25.

To be written without lifting pen from paper.

26. etc

(Mothers may continue this series.)

XV. Both feet, neither crossed nor far apart, should rest on some support.

XVI. The head should not be turned and twisted.

XVII. Now start the child writing the following copies on ruled paper, the lines being 3/8 of an inch apart from one another. Do not proceed to the following copy until the previous copy has been thoroughly mastered.

XVIII. See that all down-strokes slant in the same direction and show pressure.

XIX. See that all down-strokes belonging to the same letter are equally distant from one another.

XX. See that all letters are separated from one another by a space about twice as large as that by which down-strokes belonging to the same letter are separated.

XXI. See that words are separated from one another by a space three times as large.

XXII. Carefully attend to such minor points as placing the *i*-dot exactly over the *i*.

Drawing

I seem to hear a good, faithful, hard-working mother exclaim: "But I know nothing of art. I could not draw a straight line if I tried." Granted, but does art consist merely in being able to draw a straight line, or a curved one, for the matter of that? Or is the vivid coloring of school children's masterpieces proudly exhibited at the end of the year to be called "art" ? If so, truly there is no hope for the average mother to teach this to her children.

Do you need such directions as this, quoted from the first book of a really excellent series on art?

> On moist paper paint the blue sky half-way down. Before it is dry dip your brush in blue and yellow, and paint the far-off trees. Then paint the grass.

or this, which is infinitely worse, because it anticipates the child's observation of natural objects and their color:

Paint the shape of the pumpkin on dry paper with a yellow wash. While this color is still wet add curved strokes of red from top to bottom. Paint the stem in green.

We are so apt to associate the word art with the useless nice accomplishments, instead of with human contrivance and skill. There is as much true art in setting a room in order as in sketching an apple-tree. There is even more, for the setting of a room in order is a piece of constructive work—making a dress or making a loaf of bread is constructive. But spreading the warm colors in irregular blotches over soft-toned paper according to directions for making sunsets is not art nor science, even though comparatively well done.

All of this leads me to say that we wrongly associate the idea of training in art with the notion of voluminous instruction and practice in the use of water-colors, oil-paints, diluted inks, the production of marvelous sunsets, and impressionistic drawings. Much of what is called art instruction is but an anemic imitation, qualifying the learner to pass judgment upon things that he could not do and would never undertake. The shoemaker who set the ancient painter right with regard to some mistakes he had made in the shoe of one of his figures was not criticizing art, but was making use of his perfect knowledge of shoemaking.

Every child loves to draw, and should be permitted to do so, learning at the same time, however, that there are certain things, as walls and furniture, upon which he may not use that pencil, for the teaching of proper relationships is a part of the training in art. Give him a thick pencil or crayon in order to avoid cramping of the fingers. His first drawings will be horizontal and vertical lines connected. To him they may represent a whole menagerie. As a first exercise he may learn to print large letters like the alphabet on his blocks. Some may question the value of teaching a child to print; but viewed from the standpoint of future utility and of a child's eagerness to do this, it hardly seems wasted time.

Drawing to the child is good employment and recreation—a

good time to let him alone and see what comes of his self-activity. Then give him simple tools—pencil, rounded scissors, and jack-knife. For the child to cut from printed paper models his toys, dolls, house-forms, etc., is fairly good, as it exercises the eye and the fingers; but how much better is it for him to outline the forms himself, and cut them, giving him the right to call them truly his own!

Far more freedom will be allotted the drawing, not only freedom of action, but freedom from directions at every step. The child's unhampered drawing leads him onward, outward, upward. It brings out the inward child as writing never can. The writing-lessons are set—there is little freedom for originality—it is muscle-training, nerve-training. To be able to draw means to be able to express yourself clearly in the one universal language. As a form of self-expression drawing holds an important place in mental development. As a means of conveying ideas, if for no other reason, it may well hold an honorable place in education.

For a long time the child will represent objects by vertical and horizontal lines. Then he begins to observe a little the form which he represents by outlines. Within his reach is an inexhaustible supply of natural objects to examine as to form, color, and appearance, then to picture in his crude but satisfying fashion, a potato, an egg, a leaf, a cat-tail, a blade of grass, vegetable forms, a tree without foliage. He may outline the scissors, knife, fork, spoon. Then come such forms as a candlestick, tea-kettle, tea-pot, a carrot, rail fence, butterfly, a swallow in flight, or dozens of them; a rabbit, chair, and house represented by straight lines. He may trace the outline of a leaf, then fill in midrib and veins. He will rejoice in outlining a sail-boat, picket fence, kites, well-sweep, pump, and gate.

Rightly employed, drawing may be one of the most profitable adjuncts of education. It is most valuable when illustrative of other branches, and is a powerful aid in training the habit of observation.

X

HOW TO TEACH OBSERVATION

"EYES have you, but you see not; ears have you, but you hear not?" This kindly warning of the Great Master is timely when applied to the present generation, as it was two thousand years ago.

Most difficulties which crop up and grow in the school career of a child can be traced back to Not Seeing and Not Hearing, to the lack of Observation.

Not long ago a normal-school instructor, himself the author of one of the best text-books used in the public schools, visited an experimental school and was present at an arithmetic lesson. When he left he said: "You certainly teach arithmetic as it ought to be taught. You insist first of all that your pupils clearly understand what they hear and read when a problem is given them to solve. And therefore they find no real difficulties. You are teaching them to see and hear. My pupils, young men and women, mostly high-school graduates, have never learned to use their eyes and ears. They cannot read. If you give them fractions to add they will add the numerators; if you set them to multiply fractions they will multiply the numerators; and so on with every simple arithmetical operation. It is almost impossible to teach them. And they are to be let loose as teachers of the coming generation."

The readers of this book will therefore understand, and perhaps kindly appreciate, that the writer, considering the gravity of the subject, applied to that well-known biologist, Prof. George H. Hudson, and asked him to help in writing this chapter to the book. He consented. What he wrote follows, and is acknowledged with many sincere thanks and the highest appreciation.

"Why do so many people characterize a child as 'all ears and eyes'? Why do we so frequently utter the command, 'You must not touch that'? The psychologist answers these questions by calling our attention to the fact that the senses are the only avenues through which the mind can receive those stimuli which are essential to its development; they are the tentacles, so to speak, and the only ones, with which the child can lay hold of and attend to the outside world. How important a part may be played by a single sense like that of touch is well shown by its use in awakening and developing the mind of Helen Keller. If the senses are the only gates to the mind it must follow that the clearness, accuracy, and fullness of our knowledge must depend primarily upon the perfection of the receiving-avenues. The child's activity, then, is simply a manifestation of Nature's way of taking the first and fundamental steps in its education.

"Many parents are content to let Nature work unaided in this matter; but as certainly as we may assist her in securing a better muscular development through supervision and encouragement of proper exercise, just so certainly we may aid her in securing a higher and more perfect sense development. Well-directed sense-training for the first ten years of a child's life will then wonderfully enhance its power to discern and discriminate. The child possessing the keener and better-developed senses will, other things being equal, become the more intelligent, the happier, and the better-equipped citizen.

"Intelligent sense-training is thus one of the most fundamental or basic problems in education. It deals particularly with what we may call the physical or animal aspect of development, and it may and should begin in earliest infancy. It is thus in its very nature the work of the home, and it should be continued through all the early years of school life. Its key-words are Observation, Comparison, and Discrimination. By observation we do not mean simply seeing. We may observe through taste, touch, smell, sound, temperature, or muscular tension. All these separate gates to the mind should receive proper and adequate attention.

"As a matter of fact, our modern civilization has had a tendency to shut out the normal stimuli of sense development. First, our opening sentence is indicative of a tendency to repress Nature's efforts, and this for the purpose of personal comfort, or because of fragile and costly material which the child might injure. Individual wealth in unintelligent hands thus tends to lay the foundation for intellectual decay. Second, the four walls of a room exclude the varied songs of birds, the rustle of leaves, the music of brooks, and a thousand varied and delicate ways in which Nature appeals to the senses of higher animals. The same walls exclude the odor of balsam and pine, of ferns and flowers, and even of the fresh air itself. We may surround the child with colors, but we cannot offer the changes presented by trembling leaf, nodding flower, or moving bird — by cloud, sunset, or starlight. Uniform steam heat does not stimulate the skin as does the change from sunshine to shadow, and vice versa, or the kiss of a breeze on hands and face. Ab, on his bed of dry leaves in the open forest, was better circumstanced than our shut-in infants. We must add to the usable variety in the home, but we must not neglect over first mother—the beautiful and wonderful out of doors. To be shut off from these vast spaces and this benign influence for too many hours either in home or school is nothing less than a crime against health and future happiness. A little reflection concerning these two modern tendencies should convince us that our increasing interference with Nature's method of sense development is both real and vital. Here, too, we are introducing factors that, if allowed to remain, will most assuredly lead to racial deterioration. It is not then simply a question as to whether we shall allow Nature to use her method alone or with intelligent aid; but it involves also the question as to whether or not we shall cease our unconscious but dangerous antagonism.

"Let us look now within these gates. Through the senses the brain receives images that are stored in memory and recalled for comparison with other similar images. We thus form concepts and gain those very important groups known as apperceptive ideas. In other words, the mind is a castle of many rooms which may only be filled through experience, but the rooms themselves and the avenues to them are determined by heredity. To give a better mental inheritance after birth is an impossibility. The factor of inheritance is then fixed—its influence will persist through life—yet we should recognize it in all our efforts at education. Whether the house and its avenues be good or bad, we have control of the furnishing, for this must come through the environment, and over this factor we have almost unlimited control. The awakening mind will endeavor to select images for use in its thought-processes that its inheritance leads it to demand. We have the power, however, to present it with images that will lead to a more agreeable furnishing. 'What shall the furnishings be?' is then another fundamental question in education, and this furnishing also starts with the very first use of the developing senses.

"Again we must depend very largely on the home for this essential portion of a proper mental equipment. Again also the time spent indoors, and particularly in the school-room, involves a distinct loss in percept-collecting, and without this we cannot acquire an individual, vivid, and varied imagery. I once visited a school whose walls were bare and whose windows had the lower panes painted to prevent the children from looking out of doors. A bright little girl had a single question asked her, and in a minute it was answered. For the rest of that period she heard answers, good, bad, or indifferent, and listened to words of condemnation or praise. There was an insufferable lack of ventilation, a marked spirit of unrest, and a desire on the part of some to enliven the proceedings a bit. The second period was like unto the first, and this 'valuable discipline' was probably continued day after day, month after month, year after year. Thus this child served a prison sentence in a graded school.

She 'did time' as certainly as any convicted criminal. The result was a deadened mind and early death by consumption.

"The school's greatest effort is to develop the machinery of expression. A vast amount of time is spent on spelling, grammar, composition, rhetoric, literature, and on languages other than our own. The child's mind has been filled with choice examples of how to express himself, but he has no use for these examples, for he has no beautiful personal imagery to express. His training in the use of tools was at the expense of a rich and varied individual experience—his material to work with is not his own and therefore not vital. Shakespeare was a devoted and accurate observer of Nature and of his fellow-men. He laid in a wonderful stock of vital, personal records, and then gave expression to his wealth of mental imagery. This vivid imagery was not the product of a school. On the other hand, our vastly more elaborate system of training for ability to express thought has been used on millions of individuals, but has not produced a Shakespeare. Perhaps that is not to be expected, but we might at least expect the development of equal mental power. It is just possible that Lincoln and Edison and others became really great because they did not have the disadvantage of a modern education.

"To neglect to store the mind, through personal experience, with varied and vital images of its own is a very serious defect in school education. Our children may devour language, but they cannot digest it. One can neither impart nor comprehend anything but the commonplace unless he has a wealth of stored imagery. Every teacher of English gets enough incongruous answers to make a funny though really pathetic book. A child in an Adirondack school recently read, 'It was a moment that a painter might have seized.' A visitor asked: 'Did you ever see a painter?' 'Yes, sir,' replied the boy, 'my father shot one last winter.'

"It should be the aim to get the foundation material for mind-furnishing through personal observation of natural objects or natural phenomena. If you cannot watch the opening of a real sea-anemone or the eruption of a volcano it will be wise to go to the moving-picture. Although not real, the close facsimile will give material to impart to a friend or to enable the child to understand the written description of another. We but express organic law when we say that THE DEVELOPMENT OF THE MIND IS IN DIRECT PROPORTION TO THE VARIETY OF ITS REGISTERED AND CLASSIFIED PERCEPTS. The two great fundamentals of mind development, then, are educated senses and a furnishing of vivid, personally acquired, true, and basal ideas concerning the environment. The only possible means of securing these things is through OBSERVATION as herebefore defined.

"What I may call the third fundamental in education consists in training the power to express, and the cultivation of this power also begins with the home and the cradle. We cannot here, nor need we, emphasize the various forms through which expression may be developed. A vocabulary is, however, one of the essentials, and we may briefly point out its use as an aid in observation. If we desire a child to see more in a flower than mere surface, form, color, or odor we must reveal the pleasures of more careful or purposeful observation. Suppose we give the word 'stamen' to use in the description of a part, and follow this after some days with 'anther' and 'pollen.' Some other day we may go out to see in how many places in garden or field we may find stamens. Lead to the child's discovery of stamens on the elms and maples in early spring and on the grasses and plantains in summer. In a class of high-school graduates I have sometimes found that but one in thirty knew that pussy-willows were clusters of flowers possessing stamens. The words given are enough of the flower vocabulary to last for a year unless the child asks for other names. This same year we may plant seeds and watch their sprouting and growth. During the second year we could hunt for baby seeds. Where do you find them? Always in an 'ovary.' This is a new word, and if desired the terms 'style' and 'stigma' may be added. Where in the flower is the ovary? Are those of all blossoms alike in form? There is no need for hurry in this vocabulary, but it will lead to more careful observation and discrimination, and also allow the child to talk intelligently about the flowers of the neighborhood. Go over the whole field of your environment.

"Let the child see something of the heavens on still, clear nights. Learn the names of a number of conspicuous constellations. Not ten per cent, of our recent high-school graduates over the whole land know even what the 'milky way' is. Let the child find out through observation if the Big Dipper shifts its position. A high-school graduate recently discovered it upside down, but insisted that at her home it was always right side up, and wrote to her father for proof. If one has never contemplated the starry heavens on a clear night how can he grasp the thought of the Psalmist in, 'When I consider Thy heavens, the work of Thy fingers, the moon and the stars, which Thou hast ordained; what is man, that Thou art mindful of him?' See if the moon keeps the same star neighbors on successive days. What is the direction of her movement through the stars? Where is the sun when the moon is full, and where when she is new? Do not answer the question for the child; train him to investigate and discover.

"Our observational work must not neglect the sky by day. If a fixed vertical post is conveniently situated let the child measure, and record on a calendar, the length of its shadow about once in two weeks, and beginning some time in March or April. On the following March give him the problem of discovering the days of the year when this shadow is longest and when shortest. Afterward consult an almanac with him and see how nearly correct was his determination. These are the turning-points in the sun's apparent northward or southward motion. At them the 'sun stands' hence 'solstice.' Give him the name when convenient or perhaps after he has found the summer solstice. If he is told his error, in days, at this time, he will try to make his determination of the winter solstice more accurate.

"What changes in the air are brought about by north or south winds? Personify the winds. How do their characters differ? When fairly well understood read some of the personifications found in good literature.

"Take the whole field of nature. Visit an outcrop of rock and see if the discovery as to how soil is formed may be made. Can you find fossils in the neighborhood? What does running water do? Find miniature land forms, cations, and deltas in their making. Aim to know something of the herbs and trees, the birds and insects inhabiting the territory around home.

"We may recapitulate the aims of this observational work as follows:

"The development and training of the senses.

"The collection of a wealth of true and vivid imagery.

"The acquisition of a vocabulary of use in learning about the things around us, and a development of the power to express our ideas.

"But this is not all that we have gained. In this work we have come to make a more intimate acquaintance with our environment; we have gained knowledge of great and lasting worth; we have been led to appreciate and love the communion with nature; we have secured a wholesome measure of contentment; and we have done much toward developing a personality greatly to be desired."

The wisdom of Dr. Hudson's remarks is manifest. Yet, the mother back in the country on a farm, in the woods, is prone to think: "If we could only live in the city where my children could have the advantages of a good school!" Of her own reflection she should be able to discover how fortunate are those who spend their childhood far from the big, highly organized school. Not only have they the negative advantage of safe distance from the rattle of school machinery, but the positive blessing of opportunity to learn from Nature's self. If one would but attend the school of the woods, the college of field and orchard, the university of the farm—attend with the desire to extract therefrom the fullest lessons—he would know the beauty of intellectual health, he would gain therefrom the rugged virility and power, the originality and independence which are Nature's own certificates of promotion, not to be acquired in any more conventional surroundings, and not to be counterfeited by any amount of so-called "nature study" carried on in crowded class-rooms under the direction of a teacher only one degree less ignorant of her subject than is her class.

It is this sort of exotic training in our overcrowded schools which tends to produce the city child who does not know that there is a difference between a rock and a mountain; whose knowledge of forestry is limited to the impression that all trees can be divided into two great classes—either they are Christmas trees or they are not Christmas trees; who will ask you whether rivers flow into the ocean or the ocean into the rivers; who thinks mountains resemble eyebrows, because they look that way on the map; who would hesitate to say whether a partridge is a biped or an amphibian.

Primitive men walk through a world with eyes trained to read the faintest signs and with ears attuned to the slightest sound. Children are very close to their savage ancestors. A child's senses are not dulled by disuse and misuse. Many parents are content to let Nature work unaided in this training instead of assisting her to secure a higher and more perfect sense development. Observation cultivates interest and alertness and brings about the ability to measure, to contrast. It is the forerunner of reflection and judgment, the qualities of a mature mind.

A child has an ardent curiosity and a love of experimental inquiry. Compare for a moment the knowledge and information that we can obtain through observation, with the indispensable information that can be found only in books, and you get a better idea of the value of training the observational powers.

Just think of all a baby has to achieve, and in so short a time! The use of his limbs involves a vast and complicated series of mechanical problems. He has to become acquainted with dangers and how to avoid them; with difficulties and how to overcome them. He reads faces long before he dreams of reading books. He rapidly acquires a new language, and with such subtle touches of idiom that he can never hope to learn another language quite so thoroughly. Then he has to make acquaintance with a world as new to him as it once was strange and new to Adam. He must become acquainted with the animals and give each a name. The sun, the moon, the stars, the green old hills—all different from one another—the trees, the flowers—all these are portrayed so accurately that when other later pictures have faded and vanished these first ones return with the early freshness still undimmed.

How very few great men have spent their early boyhood in a city flat! Today's men of achievement were fifty years ago boys on the farm, and in their declining days they go back to the ancient woods with rod and reel, pipe and book, to again taste the happiness of serene repose. Many of the lessons handed down from the ancients, and vulgarly considered mere fables, are beautiful allegorical expressions of great and vital truths. Among them there is none more instructive than the legend of Antæus. Sprung from the earth, as we all are, he was invincible so long as he remained in contact with the Primal Mother; but being separated from the source of strength, he was subdued and slain. Now the Hercules that strangles us takes many names and forms; but the process is the same. He separates us from the earth; that is, he deprives us of communion with nature, which communion is of the utmost importance in building up a vigorous manhood and also gives us many of our purest pleasures.

The love of nature is deep and ineradicable in the normal human heart, and the child who has never known the ministering care of that great parent, is, in a measure, robbed of its birthright, which would have enabled it to build up a noble life.

Much has been said and written of earthly changes, but these changes are only apparent or imaginary. Individuals change; but the race remains, and, above all, the laws of development are unchangeable. We do not grow oaks in hotbeds or flower-pots; nor need we expect to see the highest types of manhood or womanhood produced in modern SOCIETY.

It was in the desert that the patriarch had the vision of angels keeping the communication between earth and heaven. In the wilderness may still be found the angels of health, peace, and contentment.

The main cause of regret is not that the child's stock of information is so woefully limited. Lack of knowledge is less to be deplored than lack of feeling. We go to Nature less to learn than to absorb. We go for enjoyment and companionship. Nature meets us half-way and takes a hold upon us that lightens the dull, dragging hours of later imprisonment within stupid walls. In speaking of his delightful essays *Wake-Robin*, John Burroughs says:

"I wrote this book sitting at a desk in front of an iron wall. I was the keeper of a vault in which many millions of bank-notes were stored. During my long periods of leisure I took refuge in my pen. How my mind reacted from the iron wall in front of me and sought solace in memories of the birds and of the summer fields and woods!"

He took refuge from his long periods of leisure!

Not every child, indeed, can live among such scenes as *Wake-Robin*, but in this day of rapid and cheap transportation it is possible for nearly every child to be trained to see and to enjoy nature at first hand. First, there are the city parks. Again, the money thrown away on picture shows would take mother and children for an afternoon trip to the near-by country. Do you not sincerely pity the boy who has never cut his own fishing-rod, set a trap, or found a bird's nest? or who needs to ask, what is a babbling brook? and who does not know of his own seeing of "the rushing of great rivers"?

There was culture before there were books, and education should first aim at culture. Mere book knowledge is not culture, nor will it produce culture. Not only does home training prepare the child for useful life and good citizenship, but it gives it a working knowledge that opens the door of understanding to academic subjects. For instance, while the girl beats the eggs and you answer her questions she gets a practical chapter in organic chemistry. Washing dishes with her mother as a teacher she finds out the properties of water, the hardness and softness; the actions of acids and alkalis as combined in soap; the effect of heat and cold on certain bodies. Was there ever a better laboratory than the kitchen to teach a girl all she need know about chemistry? She learns about mould, mildew, rust, fermentation, freezing mixtures, temperatures, salt, and baking-soda. She learns of what materials different utensils are made, and how and why that material is used. Here are more of the things a child can learn from you or with your help in the kitchen: food-stuffs, their constituents and where they come from; the making and uses of glass, pottery, iron, steel, brass, nickel, silver. Using the garden hose teaches the pressure of water. The child learns as it helps at home about coal, metals, alloys, coins, clouds, rain, snow, ice, springs, brooks, lakes, wells, canals, sea-water, salt, winds, storms, familiar animals and plants. A child who learns these and related things and uses his eyes may later on really get something worth while from a high-school course in chemistry and physics, because he knows what the book and the instructor are talking about, while the student without this home training does no more than get through the examination. The making of useful, thinking, worthy citizens depends upon the early teaching of the humble facts and duties of every-day life. The one great question in a child's mind is "What?" The importance of "How?" and "Why?" should also be firmly impressed. The habit of finding the answers to these three questions constitutes the training in observation.

Without a consistent preliminary training in observation, in the study of Nature, and the incidental learning of the facts met in every day's life, the beginners in laboratory or science classes find themselves embarrassed and confused before a striking array of information and detail, each part of which is simple enough in itself, but yet so interwoven with other information and related detail as to present a solid wall of complexity. The most necessary condition for the solution of a problem, the understanding of the data, is lacking.

Let us take the study of botany as another example. Here is a class of high-school or college students, well advanced in their teens and passably intelligent. If they are given to study a chapter on the parts of a plant, to many of them nearly every technical term used in the assignment is new and strange. Nothing seems to have a bearing upon anything else. How do they study that lesson? By a muscular effort, repeating over and over each definition and description, word for word, and holding the collection of facts securely in their memories until the desired opportunity of committing what they have memorized to a test paper.

Now consider the student who has learned to observe and trained himself to notice weeds and flowers. The assigned page is a delight to a student of this kind. The definitions are no longer meaningless, since in another style and phrasing they tell him what he has known and thought before. Does HE passively set about committing to memory the words of the text? Never. He does more. He gives their meaning, their relationships to other definitions; he puts interest and vitality into the work. He proves again and again that he who brings something to the book is the one who gets something out of it. He shows the maturity of mind that comes from long thinking. Because he has thought, he is able to face a complex assignment, whereas the beginner must deal with the single idea, which is the primitive basis. The boy or girl who has been taught to use eyes and ears is admirably fitted for scientific studies. Science is based on facts. Research does no more than classify or arrange in an orderly manner certain facts so that conclusions may be drawn. These conclusions are again and again tested by facts until research becomes science. The boy whose early life has been observant has the basis of facts and the skill in drawing conclusions needed by science. Such a boy meets with no difficulty in studying mathematics, astronomy, physics, or chemistry.

XI

HOW TO EVOLVE THE WORK HABIT

"HAST thou seen a man diligent at his work? He shall stand before kings." Since Paradise was lost to man it has been his destiny on earth to work. Education, therefore, means preparation and training for work. Without it man is not fit to live.

All must needs be educated. All are to work. By exertion of brain or sweat of brow must every child of Adam gain his daily bread if he would have it palatable, digestible, and nourishing. In that edict even he who delves may read a blessing, though its utterance sounded like a curse.

Work is the simplest solution of the problem of human happiness. An all-wise Providence has ordered that our highest enjoyments spring from our greatest necessities; and all other joys pale before the invigorating glow of satisfaction resulting from the honest performance of our duties.

Long, laboriously compiled statistical tables pretend to show that only so many hours of work per day are necessary to support life. As if to LIVE meant merely to exist, and mere existence were the end of life! Why, the animals, the reptiles, the insects, all live. Should we, the image of God, be satisfied with a life like theirs? We should, indeed, without the chastening, ennobling power of work. Toil and strife are the inalienable conditions of life on this earth; and any scheme based on elimination of these would terminate all manhood worthy of the name.

Benjamin Franklin says that the man to be envied is he who rolls up his sleeves and goes singing to his work. To gain the full benefit of our labor we must work; not merely to earn a living, but in order that, living, we may accomplish something, may become co-workers with the Creator instead of convicts carrying out our sentence. Even the panacea of four hours, two hours, or one hour a day would still be working under compulsion, and therefore slavery.

The main object of life is not knowledge, but work; the use of knowledge is to enable us to work intelligently and without loss of time. Education, to be of use, should be based on the same plan as the student's future life must be—work, strive, and win. Without work there can be neither development nor progress. We do not sufficiently value work as a means of mental development. Its possibilities are inexhaustible.

But instead of associating work and education we are apt to associate and consider inseparable books and education, so that unconsciously we define ignorance as a lack of knowledge of the few things about which we ourselves happen to know something. Even though the poor grandfather has long practiced the habits of right thinking on the elementary principles of human action, and right acting in the ordinary relations of human society, yet if he cannot parse his way to salvation he is an ignoramus to the raw mind of youth.

There were educated men, in the best sense of the word, before there were books. Between the mind that is merely a storehouse of facts and the mind well trained by hard work and hard thinking there is all the vast difference that there is between a ramshackle furniture shop and a well furnished home.

Lack of the habit of work breeds dislike of work; but work which at first seems a burdensome task in course of time becomes a pleasure. To make good citizens you must first and foremost instill in the young minds a respect for labor and create the habit of work, giving the work experience early enough for it to become a vital part of their lives. Then your children will not take their places in the ranks of the useless learned persons bringing reproach on the very name of education. Nor is it enough to teach a child how to perform certain tasks—that is a simple matter. He must be made to work. Instead of killing spontaneity compulsion prepares for spontaneity. What an effective lesson you have taught when once the learner grasps the meaning of the old, old truth—that habit grows from repeated acts, character from habit, destiny from character; that the first step is a difficult one, that continued effort brings attainment, and that every task well done is a stepping-stone to higher undertakings. These world-old truths cannot be taught by precept merely, but must be wrought into the fiber of each individual by the actual performance of physical labor. Deplorable as are the evils of child labor, they are not as far-reaching and destructive as the evils of child idleness.

To learn from books is all very well in its time and place, but that time comes after the period of learning from experience and example has well progressed. In dealing with young children it is natural and logical to form first the habit of practical work and, secondly, that of sustained mental exertion. Thus we are proceeding from the concrete to the abstract, from the known to the related unknown. All ordinary activities tend to improve the mind. Moreover, in this day of abundant literature almost any child's natural curiosity will lead him to learn to read by himself if only some one will answer his questions as to letters, words, and the meaning of words.

Two or three generations ago, when the home recognized its responsibilities and looked upon the school merely as a contributing factor in furnishing instruction, then the home and school together really educated and produced men who were types, with mind and muscle strengthened to undertake and to achieve. Where is the school that provides for boy or girl the educational advantages of the full, rich individual daily program of home life on the farm? No university course can equal in value this early all-round education without vacation. When the boy worked side by side with his father in the field and the girl did her share of the housework the problem of education was solved thus far individually and as a matter of course, and did not come up for constant public discussion. The worker at home was rarely the shirk at school, as school was then, and the old-fashioned teacher did not use such phrases as "lack of concentration," "eye-minded instead of ear-minded," in place of the more direct, if less euphonious, "The child is lazy," or "His shiftless parents have never taught him how to work."

In regard to the value of work to the individual there can be no dispute. The question is, How form the habit of work?

First, we must take account of the child's dormant sense of responsibility that may be awakened by the mere recognition of its presence, in order that the period of helplessness be not unwisely prolonged.

Secondly, we must give the small child daily regular tasks suited to his strength, increasing them with his ability to perform them.

To be sure, there is nothing novel in this, but there is not much novelty in a world as old as ours—not much that is both novel and useful. The most satisfactory pupils, taken all in all, come from homes where it is believed that every child from the age of three or four should have suitable daily tasks to perform regularly and well.

The little child should dress himself, button or lace his shoes, hang up his clothing on the proper hooks, turn the covers of his bed to air, put away his playthings when through with them, run here and there to save his mother steps about the house. As the months go by the capacity for work increases and more may well be undertaken. The beginner's assignments should be simple, for failure results more often from a confused perception of the thing to be done than from inability to accomplish what is required. There is something gratifying to every one in the feeling that he is able to do each day something more difficult than the day before. To teach the child how to work and to rejoice in a good piece of work, to make every day a little fuller and richer than the day before, to develop the child in skill, in force, in self-control—these are among the best things the very best school could hope to give, yet these things are not beyond the ken of even the busiest mother, nor are they difficult, except in so far as patience and persistent judicious attention to the undertaking are difficult for the mother herself. The problem of to-day and to-morrow is the problem of the individual child.

Many a mother will feel that she is doing her full duty in the way of fostering the work habit, and will say, "Now, what has that to do with the more complicated problem of teaching from books?" Everything. The most important outgrowth of the work habit is the power of concentration, which is the great fundamental need of scholarship. The habit of self-enforced concentration may be developed in any healthy mind if an early beginning is made. In itself a mighty conquest, it is the essential basis of further conquest. As the power of concentration is the first requisite of success, it is also the safest guarantee of success. The factors that produce and the circumstance that develop this power in the individual render a school unnecessary to that individual. Perhaps the greatest good that can be derived from a college training is the ability to intensify effort and prolong endeavor. But should not the cultivation of these valuable and all-important traits be begun before the period of college life? Not only is this accomplished with far more ease and certainty at the age of seven than at the age of twenty-one, but its early acquisition is the only assurance against waste of time and failure of achievement. The student who waits until he reaches college to learn how to work generally misses his aim. The right time to learn how to study is in the very beginning. The right way of doing so is to meet difficulties and conquer them by overcoming one at a time, and the simplest at the outset. A college diploma is of less value than the habit, the knowledge, the power "how to study." How often will a student in a preparatory or normal school take a textbook in mathematics or science or history and puzzle vainly over it by the hour, then, failing to get any sense out of it, simply labor to commit to memory the whole lesson, though not understanding it. On the contrary, the student who has had the training that begins with the thoughtful performance of simple duties, such as laying one stick square and true upon another until the wood-pile is in trim shape, making one stitch and then another until the wash-rag is knitted—all concrete tasks that can be measured and appraised with the child's singleness of vision—is enabled to take the same bothering text-book, settle himself down to it, and say to himself: "This book is written neither in Hebrew nor in Choctaw; these are English words, and any not familiar to me I shall look up in the glossary. First I shall master the first sentence; that done, I shall get the second; then, as the entire topic is made up of so many sentences, it is only a matter of perseverance for me to fit the sentences together, understand the context, and so conquer the whole."

That stock phrase of the schools, "such and such a pupil cannot concentrate," when applied to a normal child, means one of two things: an indictment of the home that has failed to train the child in habits of work, or an admission that the school work is either above or below the capabilities of the child. He can concentrate and apply energy and zeal whenever it suits him to do so to further his own interests. He digs a cave in the sand or in the snow, or builds a snow man, or dissects a toy, or builds with his blocks, wholly absorbed in that particular endeavor and working toward its completion. No dawdling over it, no half-doing, no display of weariness of soul. You watch him and say to yourself: "If he would only work as hard as that at the things he is set to at school." Unfortunately for all concerned, he has not learned the greatest and most important lesson of all—to do exactly what he is told to do. If a boy knows that when he is told to fill the wood-box it means to *fill* the wood-box; if a girl knows that when she is told to pick a cupful of berries it means to pick a cupful, not a half a cupful, that boy or girl, when set a task with books, will take for granted that they are to do that task, not sit back and depend upon some one to help them.

In the matter of the assignment of school work nearly all are working beneath their strength. Real work for a single hour accomplishes more for the student than the five or six hours of so-called study constituting a school-day. No one disputes that a small child can learn in an hour all that is worth while in the course that is now distributed over five tiring consecutive hours. He spends an hour with a book open before him, and takes great credit to himself for studying a whole hour, when in truth he has given the greater part of the time to play, dawdling over his work, enjoying neither the work nor the play. An ambition to make progress keep pace with the passing-days is more easily aroused in the beginner than after he has been a few years in the average school.

In a certain experimental school the teacher was not satisfied with the work being done by a group of ten-year-old boys. They spent the entire day in preparing assignments that could be mastered, she believed, in half the time. One morning she told this class if they could get their work finished before the usual time, three o'clock, they would be dismissed. At half past two the boys applied for permission to go home with work completed. The next morning they asked if that day the same privilege held good, and on receiving this assurance fell to work on the assignments, which were calculated to equal in difficulty the preceding day's lessons. On this second day all had finished the work by two o'clock, the time varying from ten to thirty minutes, according to the pupil. On the following morning the boys propounded this question: "If we finish our work in the forenoon, may we stay away from school this afternoon?" and were assured that they might do so. Every boy finished his work before the noon intermission. Again on the fourth morning was the experiment repeated, with the result that the slowest of this group was enabled to make a triumphant departure by eleven o'clock.

Then a strange thing happened. When school was resumed for the afternoon these boys presented themselves, looking rather sheepish at being found around a school-house when not compelled to appear, and explained their presence by saying, "There was nothing doing around home." The teacher had discovered two things: first, these boys really could do well in two hours the work upon which they had been spending five hours; second, the day on which these children had learned what it meant to work to the very limit of their capacity was the day on which school possessed for them attractions to draw them back.

XII

HOW TO TEACH THE RETARDED CHILD

IN countries where public instruction has been carried on for centuries, where mature experience has made parents and teachers wiser, it has become a well-established and recognized fact that there must be a certain percentage of failures in the attempt to pass the growing generation successfully through a scholastic system. Such natural and irremediable failures we can only meet with the question: "What can be done to enable the intellectually handicapped child to become a useful citizen, and what is the teachable maximum?"

Very different, and sadly different, is it with the poor child that, though naturally well equipped for a successful school course, is not only retarded, but dulled and stunted by avoidable hindrances and checks due to blighting and blasting influences of home and school. Here the only efficient help can come from the mother, who, realizing her grave responsibility and bounden duty, resolutely takes matters into her own hands and remedies what has been spoiled by her own negligence and the culpable inefficiency of teacher and school.

The following instances, taken from Swift's *Mind in the Making*, will prove to her that she need not be dismayed in facing what may have seemed to her a hopeless task, and give her hope, courage, patience, and strength to accomplish it successfully.

The great Swedish botanist, Carl Linnaeus, who invented that wonderful system of classifying plants, so impressed the directors and teachers of the "gymnasium" with his worthlessness and backwardness that his father "was advised to make a cobbler of him, as he was quite unfit for any learned profession. Yet all the time the boy was lost in the undergrowth of thoughts which in their maturity were to revolutionize the study of botany."

Charles Darwin "was considered a very ordinary boy, rather below the common standard of intellect."

Sir Isaac Newton "showed so little ability that at fifteen he was taken out of school and set at work upon a farm."

"Robert Fulton was a dullard because his mind was filled with thoughts about other things than his studies; but his teachers could not understand this, and so the birch-rod became a frequent persuader."

"Alexander von Humboldt said of himself 'that in the first years of childhood his tutors were doubtful whether even ordinary powers of intelligence would be developed in him, and that it was only later in boyhood that he began to show any evidence of mental vigor."

"The hatred of Joseph Banks, the English naturalist, for the monotony of school routine was so marked as to bring complaint from his teachers. Yet it was not dislike for work; he simply could not travel the road by which alone the educational doctors would permit him to reach the golden gate."

"John Hunter, the celebrated anatomist and surgeon, is reported by one writer to have been unable to read or write at seventeen years of age, so great was his hatred for school. In his unappreciated condition of learned ignorance he just missed becoming a cabinet-maker through the fortunate failure of his brother-in-law, in whose carpenter shop he was working."

"Oliver Goldsmith's teacher, in his early childhood, thought him one of the dullest boys she had ever tried to teach. She said he was 'impenetrably stupid'; she was afraid that nothing could be done for him. His indolence and dislike for his university tutor, who called him ignorant and stupid before his classmates, combined to make him hate mathematics, science, and philosophy."

"Henry Ward Beecher at ten years of age, according to his sister, Mrs. Stowe, 'was a poor writer, a miserable speller, with a thick utterance, and a bashful reticence which seemed like stolid stupidity. He was not marked by the prophecies even of partial friends for any brilliant future. He had precisely the organization which often passes for dullness in early boyhood."

"Spencer's native antagonism to the rote method was so intense that it prevented him from making any substantial progress during his school course in the grammar of his own or foreign languages. His mind was on the non-conforming sort, as indeed all superior minds are, and school organization has not yet been sufficiently perfected to take them into account."

Did you ever meet the boy of ten, who has been in school the last four years, covering no more ground than he might have done in six months, who has been placed in the third grade when he really was fit only for the first, so far as the quality of his work was concerned? He has felt unhappy and wretched in school, and has acquired such a hatred of books and study and school and teachers that his case seems entirely hopeless. His temper is soured. He seems to feel that if he is only hateful enough, and can make himself disagreeable enough, the teacher will give up in despair. He kicks the chairs, smashes his pencil in bits, hides his book so as to necessitate loss of time in recovering it.

Under a special plan of instruction the first six months' work seems productive of no results except to convince him that the prescribed hour's work has to be attained before he will be dismissed, even if it takes four hours, as it frequently does. The latter part of the year he commences to work, makes such advancement that you dare not trust your senses, qualifies for the examination, and passes the public-school test admitting him to the sixth grade the coming year. His former teachers are astounded as well as disdainful, but take him into the grade, prophesying, however, that he will only be demoted at the end of the month, as he will never be able to keep up. However, his work is never quite poor enough to warrant his demotion, although at the end of the year he is retained in the grade.

Now, the boy who does not go forward is unquestionably going backward, and after such an experience it takes a long time to enliven any ambition.

One drawback is sometimes a limited vocabulary. Sometimes its range is confined to sporting terms, the jargon of athletics, and the slang of the street.

His imagination maybe weak. Geography and history, then, are only a matter of words.

But intellect and mental capacity are not gaged by school standards, just as school standards do not insure a standard of efficiency. In the Dishwashers' Union of San Francisco one member out of every seven is said to be a college graduate. Most of these men attribute their present lowly position to the fact that their school and college training was not adequate to their requirements. But as one of them shrewdly observed: "Our early training was at the root of it. The child properly trained during the years when parental control can most powerfully assert itself will not go through college and become a dishwasher."

Before suggesting how to treat and teach the backward or retrograded child we ought to analyze the causes of such backwardness or retrogression. These are of three kinds: Physical, mental, and local—*i. e.*, caused by unfavorable environment.

The physical causes, as adenoids, defective eyesight and hearing, anemia, malnutrition, and such like, can only be dealt with by a physician, to whose attention they must be brought by the watchful mother or teacher.

The mental causes are principally: Lack of self-control, lack of memory, an abnormally slow process of mind-maturing, complete absorption in some line of thought entirely outside of the school curriculum.

Self-control, the principal aim, and—when achieved—the triumph of education, includes the habits of regular, patient, persevering work and of concentration at will. The immature mind can hold itself to the one thought but a few minutes. Then it gradually learns to control thought as it controls muscles, and so to hold the mind for a longer and longer period to the one set task as the powers of the mind unfold. By false mental training this power, or as much of it as the child has acquired at play, is impaired. Many grown people can concentrate only at play. They retain the child mind.

With many a new pupil the teacher's work for weeks and months is undoing what has been done in the wrong way—going back to the very beginning and disentangling the confused threads of an encumbering weave, combating a dislike and dread of what should have been a delight.

No matter how stupid a child has come to believe himself to be, you can persuade him that there is some work meant for him which he can do better than any one else in the world—that he has some gift whose development will lead to a happy, useful existence. Train him to see that:

> "I am only one.
> But still I am one.
> I cannot do everything.
> But still I can do something.
> And because I cannot do everything
> I will not refuse to do the something that I can do."

There must be no quitting work when the whistle blows. Insist that a good piece of work be accomplished each day before the quitting-time can be considered.

The first requisite in this training of the discouraged child is to give him faith in his own possibilities. Give tasks suited to his strength. Mastering one thing is better than attempting many things and mastering none. Let the pupil have the sense of victory over one subject, and he will attack others with a confidence that assures another conquest. It is this sense of achievement that makes the boy, or for all that the man, feel that he is somebody, and that his life is after all worth while.

Make use of homely examples, as the Tortoise and the Hare. Tell him of the spider that spun his web seven times as it was successively destroyed. Show him that the noblest undertakings in all history have been completed only by hard labor, under adverse conditions, that ultimate triumph is ours only through the effort to make each day a round in the ladder of success. On the whole, and with tactful modifications, the method and plan, as given in the chapters relating to reading, spelling, and arithmetic, should be followed; but we shall give here some concrete examples of how to teach these to the backward child. The boy who comes from school laden with home work in arithmetic might be given one of the exercises each evening for five minutes. A single month's training will make him a quicker worker.

The mother may discover that her child of ten years or more, after spending several years in school, is a failure so far as arithmetic is concerned. He does not know the multiplication tables, he cannot solve mentally the simplest problems. Confused by the teaching received, he has great difficulty in applying his mind to an assigned task; he does not give attention, he cannot concentrate. Now it is not an easy matter to take in hand a pupil who has reached the point of hating study, of despairing of his own power of accomplishment. He must first learn that steady work will overcome difficulties and increase his power to work. No other subject seems quite so available for this purpose as arithmetic.

The plan for number work outlined for beginners may well be followed with the twelve-year-old backward child, the material difference being in the teacher's attitude. It is now a different mind with which she must deal, and the task is complicated by the confused mass of undigested information and notions in the pupils brain. But, while the task is difficult, it is by no means hopeless, and, since it cannot be done in school, it must be done by the mother or a special instructor. We shall use objects here, as for the younger pupils, yet their use need not be so long continued. Also we shall use a scheme that is out of place with the little child, because of the danger of over-stimulation. This is the practice of timing the pupil, marking in his book the length of time needed for a piece of work, dating it, and day after day testing to note the gain in speed.

For example, ask him to count to 100 by twos, timing him. The first count may, in some cases, require three to five minutes. Note this, explaining to the pupil that each time he does this he may expect the task to become easier. Again he tries, and perhaps reaches 100 in half the previous time. Now his interest is aroused; he is learning to work. He gives attention to this as he would to a game of marbles. The record in his book might appear thus:

COUNTING TO 100 BY TWOS

September 5th.

1st time	3 min	
2nd "	1 "	40 sec.
3rd "	1 "	

September 6th.

1st time	50 sec
2nd "	40 "
3rd "	35 "

The counting backward by twos from 100 may be taken in the same way; and so may the succeeding addition tables be treated. This is mainly for the purpose of pinning his attention to his work. This plan has value because the pupil is striving to improve his own record. But rapidity is not the main object. Accuracy comes first. The pupil is first to be sure, then quick. If he makes a single mistake the exercise is a failure. Let him at once stop there and begin all over again.

Most teachers have noticed how difficult it seems to teach a child the multiplication table as he gets older. It is one of the things learned far more easily at nine than at twelve. For this reason we shall change somewhat the order of work outlined, and instead of learning the multiplication tables immediately after addition the pupil will work steadily at measuring numbers, as

$$18 \div 3 =$$
$$18 \div 4 = \text{etc.}$$

going as rapidly as his ability seems to justify. From one half-hour to an hour a day may well be spent at this. Then after a few weeks stress may be laid upon the multiplication tables. So much for arithmetic.

The child of ten or thereabouts who hitherto has not made satisfactory progress in learning to spell and read may start afresh, beginning with the first of the following lessons. In spelling, however, as in arithmetic, the plan of dealing with a six-year-old can rarely be successfully followed with one several years older, especially if the latter has been gorged with lessons. While this older child is learning words, according to the lists given, the following plan should be pursued. If judiciously carried out it will tend to improve his spelling and English and to promote habits of concentration.

Take Longfellow's poem, "The Builders," which begins:

> All are architects of fate,
> Working in these walls of time;
> Some with massive deeds and great,
> Some with ornaments of rhyme.

Tell the child to study the first line until he can write it correctly from memory. At the outset this will not be easy, although there is but one hard word. Let the pupil at first take his own time to study the words before attempting to reproduce them. If a single error is made he must study the line again and write it anew. A single line may be sufficient for the first lesson, especially if real difficulty is experienced by the novice. The next day he will study the second line in the same way. As this will be mastered with more ease, the pleased child will welcome the opportunity to try another.

After a few weeks of this training the pupil is usually able to learn and reproduce a whole stanza in the time at first required for a single line. The lessons, as mentioned before, should always be dated and measured in order to have a record of progress. Increased ability to memorize may easily enable the same pupil after a few months to reproduce correctly a considerable number of stanzas, such as that given, in the time at first required for one.

What has been said of training the backward child individually may apply to a great extent to the teaching of a class which has been poorly grounded. The main idea is to attempt but little at first, but to require such plain and definite results that even the child can notice them and must be impressed by them. To give an illustration: A teacher took up her duties in a remote country school of a single room, and there faced a disheartening state of affairs. The children, large and small, had been so wretchedly trained that there was no foundation of knowledge whatsoever, and no starting-point, but a new start had to be made by each and all. To teach reading, spelling, writing, and arithmetic all in one year and bring the pupils forward in accordance with their ages reminded her of Caesar, who had to do so many things at the same time. The undertaking was so formidable that the teacher decided to start by teaching but one thing, in the belief that this would be better than attempting all and getting nowhere. She chose writing. The children wrote copies all day long, with frequent intermissions, and were delighted to find at the close of the first day that they could do better than in the morning. Some had learned to write but a single letter, others merely noted the improvement on the first copy. They wrote steadily for three weeks. In that time they made greater improvement than would ordinarily have been made in two years of slipshod practice. Furthermore, the children beheld with delight the marvelous gain, and for the first time knew the fruits of sustained endeavor. Because the progress was easily marked writing in itself was a fortunate choice for a beginning.

The next subject taken up in practically the same way was arithmetic. This, alternating with penmanship, was continued until a safe and profitable beginning had been made. Long lessons on the one subject, merely stopping for frequent outdoor intermissions, were not tiring to the children. After all, the wisdom of the saying, "Change of occupation is rest," is as questionable as that of so many catchy phrases. It becomes foolish if carried to extremes.

Then came the spelling, on which now the stress of work was placed, while writing and arithmetic occupied shorter periods. The children came to learn half a dozen spelling-lessons in a day; interest was at high tide. Every child worked as hard and fast as he could. At the close of the year such progress had been attained that the usual year's work in the regulation school could not be compared to it.

The once-awakened and ever-increasing interest which each child felt in his own manifest progress successfully combated the previously uncontrollable and obstinate absorption in some injurious line of thought of his own choosing, quickened the process of mind-maturing, and provided the much-wanted stimulus to mental growth.

Sympathetic understanding of the backward children's needs and an utter absence of hurtful environment had done the rest.

"The stone that the builders rejected, the same is become the headstone of the corner."

XIII

AIDS FOR HOME TEACHING

Note-Books

THE child should have a composition-book for all written work. Although a comparatively short time will be given daily to written lessons, yet the way in which these are planned and executed will have an important bearing upon mind-training and the formation of good habits. A few rules may be of service in the beginning:

1. Do not hurry the child in his writing. A single line representing his very best effort is worth something. It represents creative power. A whole page embodying carelessness or indifference would better not have been written.
2. No written work should be thrown away. No lessons should be prepared on loose paper that will shortly reach the waste-basket. The destination of the work is too apt to influence its character.
3. Each day's work should be an improvement over that of the preceding day. Make this fact impressive. Teach him in this book the truth of the old saying that repeated acts form habit, habits make character, and character determines destiny.

If each day's work is better than the last the child will see that a week represents notable improvement, and that a month's work sometimes produces a transformation. Previous work with its mistakes and imperfections is before his eyes as a reminder to eliminate these imperfections. Little by little the young child will learn to regard as important the appearance of his book—he will keep margins, attend to the size and uniformity of the letters, and avoid blots. Since erasures are not tolerated, he must take increasing pains.

There are few more pernicious habits than that of preparing written lessons in a slovenly manner—the sure result when no special value is attached to the written page. The cost of neat composition-books may possibly amount to something more than would the reams of cheap paper, yet they acquire a value that makes them worth keeping permanently and worth putting one's best efforts upon.

Thus the child is early trained in valuable habits. He takes pride in the work of his hand. He compares his work at different periods with his own earlier work and with models, and judges as to the gain. More than all else he strives to improve upon his own record, a higher incentive than merely trying to get ahead of somebody else.

For the beginner a single note-book of the ten-cent kind is sufficient. In this he will keep all his written lessons of each day, somewhat after this fashion. To-day's lesson may be to write a few lines from "Hiawatha":

> By the shores of Gitche Gumee,
> By the shining Big-Sea-Water,
> Stood the wigwam of Nokomis.

The child intends to illustrate this lesson, and so practices the drawing of the wigwam until at least it will not be mistaken for something else. In the drawing we must deviate from the rule just given. He will practice many times on bits of paper, since this is an undertaking in which he is eager to excel. Then in his book he draws the wigwam, and underneath in his best writing he copies the two or three appropriate lines. Now the book has become a thing of wondrous beauty to the small beginner. Never fear but that he will try to make the next lesson and the next one still more beautiful.

In another part of his book he may keep whatever written spelling you give him, where he will occasionally compare the assignments as to length and difficulty, and so measure his growing powers. In still another section he writes the arithmetic tables as he works them out with the pebbles. He is learning not to crowd his work in an unsightly manner.

For the child who can already read and write there may be several note-books. One may be devoted wholly to penmanship, one to arithmetic, and one to whatever poetry and stories are written. While every book will be artistic because it represents good work according to one's gifts, yet a fourth book for the child of eight or nine may become a treasury of beauty and art. By the time the pupil is ready for this book he keeps an attractive page and has a liking for good literature. So this note-book may well be of a better quality than the others, preferably a loose-leaf book with a stiff black cover. Book and paper sufficient for a year will cost about seventy cents.

While individual taste will largely decide the matter and manner of this book, one mode of arrangement, the work of a girl of eight, is here described. It is kept for the real gems of literature that the child loves and learns.

This book has on the fly-leaf, written by a teacher, the child's name and address and the date when the book was started. On the first page is pasted an American flag in colors, carefully cut from a July magazine, and underneath begins the song "America," continuing on the reverse side. On the next page, in the center, appears a picture in sepia of a bust of Christopher Columbus, and the announcement, "Notes on American History." On the reverse page are two more small pictures, showing the departure of Columbus on his western voyage, and on the next page begins the splendid poem of Joaquin Miller's, "Columbus." A space of fully two inches is left at the top of the page for the title of this poem, and with it the illustration—an ink sketch of a gallant vessel in full sail, which, simple as it is, seems to call aloud to one, "Sail on, sail on, and on!" On succeeding pages are more pictures, about two by two and a half inches, illustrating scenes in the subsequent career of the great explorer, with a few explanatory notes written by the child, facts gleaned from the teacher or the book. Not for a moment should this be called *history*. It is merely part of the poem's great lesson.

Farther on the child has written Tennyson's "Bugle Song," illustrating it herself by copying in ink a stately castle. Then for some time appear the poems that the child liked well enough to voluntarily memorize—Longfellow's "The Arrow and the Song," Tennyson's "The Shell," and at the beginning of the latter an excellent drawing of a spiral shell. Then, seemingly in the mood for shells, she has written Holmes's "Chambered Nautilus." Then comes "The Skeleton in Armor," which it seems had fascinated the child, and Tennyson's "Charge of the Light Brigade."

Fine pictures in beautiful tones on almost any subject may be obtained from different companies (especially the Perry Picture Co., Boston, or the Geo. P. Brown Co., Beverly, Mass.). The mother should write these companies for catalogues. The range and number of the pictures, as well as their low price (from one-half to two cents a piece) may well be termed marvelous.

Even the successful pasting of these pictures, placing them accurately on the page, judging of effectiveness of position, and using the paste without smearing, requires considerable skill for a child. He must also paste the little paper rings (which may be purchased at a stationery store) around the apertures in the page, to prevent the leaf tearing from the steel fasteners.

A child takes pride in the neat appearance, orderly arrangement, and valuable contents of this book. Certain principles of art are also inoculated. The child learns that there is beauty in the severe straight line, and that cheap things are overdone, overcurved, and overgilded.

Anagrams

For a small sum you can purchase boxes containing several sets of the alphabet printed on one side of cardboard squares. With them are directions for playing games of word-building. These letters are neater in appearance than the home-made ones, yet the making of the latter possesses the great advantage of giving the child something profitable to do. He may hunt out large letters in old magazines, carefully cut them out and paste them on the inch squares of cardboard that he has marked off and cut out with your assistance.

Poetry

No other single volume of the mother-teacher's library can quite take the place of Longfellow's poems. This book is indispensable to the American child. Indeed, if his whole literature until the age of ten were drawn from this book, not only would he be far from intellectually poor, but he would also have an indisputably good foundation for future literary studies, far better, indeed, than if he were supplied with dozens of the modern books written expressly to fit the child's understanding.

Longfellow is unquestionably the children's poet, the poet of the home and the heart. Not a line has he written that, dying, he could wish to blot. To know well a single great writer is to acquire a feeling of kinship for all great writers, and this feeling is greatly fostered in the child by giving him for his very own this book.

Note the remarkable range of material, beginning with the epic "Hiawatha," which in itself varies from the reach of comprehension of the five-year-old to fit the taste of the mature student. Then you may choose for the little one such poems as "The Wreck of the *Hesperus*," "The Children's Hour," "Village Blacksmith," "The Arrow and the Song," and "The Rainy Day," suited extremely well to children of eight or thereabouts. Next we have "The Builders" "The Bridge," "Paul Revere's Ride," and "The Day is Done." After these the child will be able to comprehend the "Courtship of Miles Standish," when read to him by the mother; and, lastly, we have the creation that belongs at the very pinnacle of American literature, "Evangeline." To so rear a child until he reads with pleasure the magnificent selections last named will school him to read intelligently other authors that without such preliminary training would be incomprehensible.

If there can be but one volume of the modern writers in the home school, let that one be Longfellow: if two, add to it Tennyson's poems. For the small child there are two exquisite poems:

"What Does Little Birdie Say?" and "Sweet and Low." The nine-year-old will like "The Brook," which gives him many new words, a widened physiographical vista, and something for contemplation in the refrain:

> For men may come and men may go,
> But I go on for ever.

Especially the girl of nine will learn "Blow, Bugle, Blow," and "Break, Break, Break." Both boy and girl will learn "The Charge of the Light Brigade," with its striking illustration of unswerving obedience. At the very close of his life, at the threshold of eternal childhood, Tennyson wrote his immortal poem, "Crossing the Bar." When this poem is properly read to children, they will seldom express a distaste for it or a lack of inclination to make it their own.

In the "Idylls of the King" we see the adventures of King Arthur's Knights told in the wonderful word-painting of a master mind. This is not easy or light reading, but it well repays the mother to study it closely that she may later give it to the children. You are always safe in choosing Tennyson for his poetry, sanity, morals, and scientific accuracy.

Macaulay wrote few poems for children, but some are well worth while. "Horatius at the Bridge" gives a taste for Roman history, and it gives the child an agreeable introduction to this great man. They come later to his essays as to the discourse of an old friend.

Every child may learn "The Mountain and the Squirrel," by Emerson, and many of them will listen intelligently to the serious poem, "Good-By, Proud World."

Browning did a kindness to childhood in writing the "Pied Piper of Hamelin," and in connection with this one may safely point the moral and illuminate it with examples of the everyday kind —if you dance you must pay the fiddler.

Joaquin Miller has given us a lesson in "Columbus." This may be memorized by the child of ten or younger.

J. G. Holland's "Gradatim" may well be learned word for word:

> Heaven is not reached at a single bound,
> But we build the ladder by which we rise
> From the lowly earth to the vaulted skies,
> And we mount to the summit round by round.

Now and then a child of nine or ten will be interested in the forms of poetical composition. Such a one will gladly learn Milton's wonderful "Sonnet on His Blindness," and at the same time learn the structure of a sonnet—"a little song, usually of fourteen lines." But few sonnets come within the range of young pupils.

What ten-year-old country lad will fail to like and understand Whittier's "Snowbound," "Barefoot Boy," and "In School Days"? Requiring perhaps a little finer comprehension, yet again not beyond the appreciation of country boy or girl, is Lowell's "Vision of Sir Launfal," and the passage "A Day in June" they should learn by heart. Even the little ones may learn Lowell's "First Snowfall."

Another genial American poet in whom we may well strive to create a lively interest is Holmes. "Old Ironsides" goes in the list of stirring patriotic poems, while "The Chambered Nautilus" should not merely be saved for highschool classes. Instead of telling you at what age to give these fine things to the children let it be said once for all that the best way is to try them one and another on the child, giving him each unless he specifically rejects it.

To stir patriotism read to the children, not once, but once in a while, E. E. Hale's "Man Without a Country." They may learn every word of Scott's

> Breathes there the man with soul so dead—

Take the stirring verses of "The Flag Goes By." At this age every nerve will thrill in response to

> Blue and crimson and white it shines,
> Over the steel-tipped, ordered lines;
> Hats off! the colors before us fly.
> But more than the flag is passing by.

Fairy Stories

Fairy tales and twilight stories are among the inalienable rights of every child. That is not true education which neglects to train the feelings and imagination. Unfortunate is the child whose infancy has never known Cinderella, Jack and the Bean Stalk, Jack the Giant-Killer, Aladdin and his Wonderful Lamp, Ali Baba and the Forty Thieves, Blue Beard, Sindbad the Sailor, Ugly Duckling, Three Bears, and Tom Thumb. These tales, beautifully illustrated by Peter Newell, are in *Favorite Fairy Tales*, a selection of the favorite stories of various distinguished men and women. There is a smaller book of selections by Ada Van Stone Harris, *Favorites from Fairyland*. Another book of selections, *Famous Stories Every Child Should Know,* gives us several masterpieces —Ruskin's "King of the Golden River," Hawthorne's "Great Stone Face," Hale's "Man Without a Country," Ouida's "Nurnberg Stove."

If still more books are to be chosen, *Alice in Wonderland* is a perennial delight, and *Through the Looking Glass* follows closely. There are editions of both illustrated by Peter Newell. Andersen and Grimm are familiar classics. Kingsley's *Water Babies* is liked by most children.

Books

There are so many books that the mother will enjoy reading aloud to the children from time to time—not alone for the poetry or the story, but as a foundation for future intelligent progress — that it is difficult to choose among them. There are too many books, and if driven to make a choice it would be better to read nothing than to attempt to read everything.

However, we want every child to know the love of books. Then in later years, when the world's poetry turns to colorless prose, he can go to these silent friends and by their aid reconstruct in fair form the beauty and joys of vanished days and buried dreams. What better way to nourish this love of books than for the mother to gather the children about her in the long winter evenings and read to them and talk over with them the legacy of great minds? Take such stories as "Rip Van Winkle" and "The Legend of Sleepy Hollow" from Irving's *Sketch Book*, written in the inimitable style of that great author. They breathe the very spirit of those far-off days of colonial life along the Hudson's banks; they could not possibly have been written by any but one who had spent his childhood amid these very scenes.

Quite different is such a book as Chapin's *The Story of the Rhinegold*, written for those who would know the legends on which are based the music dramas of Wagner's Nibelungenleid.

Again we have *The Prince and the Pauper*, by Mark Twain, a story of the prince who became Edward VI. and a street waif who for a time change places. Two small books of selections from Mark Twain have been made for children — *Travels at Home* and *Travels in History*. A similar book of selections from the works of William Dean Howells is entitled *Boy Life*.

Or we may take Hawthorne's *Wonder Book*, in which are elaborated the Greek myths. Not a book to be hurried over, since the difficult wording here and there needs elucidation. One who reads this understandingly will want to know Greek history, since the history of Greece has its very roots and part of the trunk embedded in mythology.

As a reference book for literature, as well as for the fascinating contents of the book itself, the mother will find useful Bulfinch's *Age of Fable*, The story of the Iliad and of the Odyssey may be found well written in cheap editions.

If one would have books that will hold spellbound the ten-year-old, we have *Bold Robin Hood and His Outlaw Band* and *Robinson Crusoe* both illustrated by Louis Rhead, who has also illustrated beautiful editions of *Swiss Family Robinson*, *Gulliver's Travels*, and *Tom Brown at Rugby*. To complete the happiness of the young outlaw, give him Stevenson's *Treasure Island*, a pirate story without profanity.

If with the foregoing in the home we place *Tales of the Arabian Nights*, and some of the works of Jules Verne, surely the youthful mind will not lack stimulus.

Other classics that the mother would place within the child's reach are Shakespeare's *Merchant of Venice* and *Julius Cæsar*. In the Autobiography of Benjamin Franklin we have the shrewd wisdom of the kindly philosopher and genius, whose maxims of practical economy should be instilled in every child:

> A small leak sinks a great ship.
>
> For want of a nail the shoe was lost;
> For want of a shoe the horse was lost;
> For want of a horse the rider was lost.

Text-Books

The best text-books for children under ten are the best child literature, like "Hiawatha." There should be on hand a good dictionary, which the child should learn to use at an early age. There may well be readable histories of Greece, Rome, England, and America. *The Children's Plutarch*, by F. T. Gould, in two volumes—*Tales of the Greeks and Tales of the Romans*—is most valuable in its ethical quality, as well as its storytelling interest. Among stories of primitive life are *The Story of Ab*, Kipling's Jungle Books, and Du Chaillu's *The Country of the Dwarfs*. A well-written geography, such as Tarr and McMurry's, can be included in the home library. Two valuable little books which indicate the relation of geography to life and industry are Monroe and Buckbee's *Our Country and Its People* and *Europe and Its People*. Great care must be taken, however, in explaining maps. Children's minds become very much confused by wall-charts and maps in books.

For nature study you will want to possess Hodge's *Nature Study and Life* for study and reference; also Gibson's *Sharp Eyes*, which gives in winning fashion the procession of nature month by month, teaching us to see with loving eyes the many every day things we have been passing by as commonplace. Gibson's *Secrets Out of Doors* is a small but delightful book of selections designed particularly for young children.

Quite readable, too, and scientifically accurate, is Comstock's *Ways of the Six-footed*, describing butterfly, bee, ant, wasp, caterpillar, caddis-fly, seventeen-year locust, and mosquito.

But of good books on nature study there is an abundance. *Upland and Meadow*, by Abbot, is especially charming to the dweller in and near New Jersey, with its neighborly rambles. Ingersoll's *Wild Life in Orchard and Field* tells us not only of the birds, but also of such acquaintances as the woodchuck, squirrel, and weasel. Two charming nature studies for children are *Little Busybodies* and *A Holiday with the Birds*, by Miss Jeannette Marks and Miss Moody.

Harper's Guide to Wild Flowers, by Mrs. Caroline A. Creevey, recently published, presents the latest scientific agreement upon names and classification, and affords three methods of identification—by color, by habitat, and by seasons. All this is aided by many colored plates and drawings.

While history and geography are constantly in the making, and while the truth of today is the superstition of to-morrow, it is a restful thought that we at least have constant friends in the stars and flowers. Above all the heavens should claim our study and understanding, since whatever knowledge we may gain of them is with us and pulsating to the end of our days. Where is there a subject that will fill a child's soul as does astronomy? The humble shepherds of Chaldea, lying wakeful on the hillsides, watched the stars rise and set and knew astronomy as we do not. Little wonder they were thinkers and poets. Little wonder that we have impoverished imaginations when not one person in a hundred can tell the hour by the sun, or knows that the stars hold a steady course across the sky. There is no greater reproach than this to modern methods of instruction.

The little book by Martin, *The Friendly Stars*, is written within a child's comprehension and vocabulary, and will enable him to identify the chief stars and constellations. Through its use he may be led to the desire for more scientific lore.

As a wholesome tonic, if you have been reading such animal traits as were never known, get Burroughs' sane and kindly *Ways of Nature*. In fact, you would be glad to own all this naturalist's series.

Current Literature

There are several magazines which will be helpful. On the farm the children should have the *Country Gentleman*, which makes them feel the great worth, dignity, and opportunity of farm life and directs most practically the seasonal activities from week to week. *The National Geographic Magazine* is a monthly containing wonderful illustrations of the four comers of the globe. Thus one keeps in touch with recent discoveries, undertakings, and happenings of worldwide interest. It is not written in child language, but at the least the pictures are perfectly comprehensible to the very young. One may be sure of the *Youth's Companion* and *St. Nicholas* containing no objectionable features.

Books for Mothers

Among the well-known books on pedagogy are a few that will be valuable and interesting to every mother, written in the plain concrete style that we all like when looking for help and counsel. William Hawley Smith has given us two such human documents, *The Evolution of Dodd*, in which we see boys—real boys—depicted, and also teachers that are very genuine. A later book is *All the Children of All the People*, in which we are given sound educational doctrine, as in the sayings of the old engineer: "No man is really well educated who is not 'onto his job.'"

In *The Century of the Child*, by Ellen Key, there is food for thought concerning the home and school. Especially good is much of the chapter on "The School of the Future." Another book that will help give mothers a clear idea of the possibilities of home teaching is *The School in the Home*, by Berle, whose own children proved his theory correct by being fitted for college at the age most students enter high school. Professor Swift gives us in the first chapter of *Mind in the Making* a remarkable summing-up of the lives of the men and women who had great influence during the past century, every one of the fifty having been a failure in childhood from the standpoint of the school. The book is an interesting study of the relation of the human individual to standardized education. *Helping School Children*, by Elsa Denison, shows how parents can aid from outside the school.

As an introduction to the methods of Montessori, now commanding so much thoughtful interest, we have a readable little book by Dr. Theodate L. Smith, *The Montessori System in Theory and Practice*.

For parents who have time and energy for deeper study of the science of education, in theory and practice, we have such literature as Spencer's *Education*, Rousseau's *Emile*, Huxley's *Science and Education*, Dr. Eliot's *Educational Reform*, *Aspects of Child Life and Education*, by G. Stanley Hall, Dr. Smith, and others, Dewey's *How We Think*, McMurry's *How to Study* and *Standards of Elementary Education*, and Neff's *Power Through Perfected Ideas*. Another helpful volume is *The Normal Child and Primary Education*, by Gesell.

We also hope that every modern mother reads *Keeping Up with Lizzie*, by Irving Bacheller; *Emmy Lou*, by G. M. Martin; and Myra Kelly's *Little Citizens*.

Dr. Woods Hutchinson writes authoritatively on the health of a child.

Buy no book that claims to have no more than an ephemeral value; buy nothing that can yield its full cultural store at one harvesting. Distinguish between what is transitory and what is eternal. Primary text-books in most cases are an abomination. Ask yourself: "Shall I be willing to give space to this book on my shelves for the next ten years—twenty years?" *Mother Goose*? Yes. *Longfellow*? Yes. *Robinson Crusoe*? For a lifetime. The Jones-Mallory-Squibbs Arithmetic for Primary Grades? To the ash-barrel with it.

Said Ruskin: "No book is worth anything that is not worth much; nor is it serviceable until it has been read and reread, and loved and loved again, and *marked*, so that you can refer to the passages you want in it, as a soldier can seize the weapon he needs in an armory, or a housewife can bring the spice she needs from her store."

Made in United States
North Haven, CT
10 May 2023